Surveillance

Other titles in the
Crime Scene Investigations series

12/10/08

Surveillance

by Andrew A. Kling

LUCENT BOOKS
A part of Gale, Cengage Learning

GALE
CENGAGE Learning

Detroit • New York • San Francisco • New Haven, Conn • Waterville, Maine • London

The author wishes to thank Thomas C. Christenberry, Jay Gelber, Steve Morgan, and Mitch Pilkington for their generosity in helping me with this project. In addition, thanks go to my wife for inspiring me to take on new challenges and for putting up with my deadline aggravations, and to my parents for instilling in me the love of the art of the written word.

For more information, contact
Lucent Books
27500 Drake Rd.
Farmington Hills, MI 48331-3535
Or you can visit our Internet site at gale.cengage.com

LIBRARY OF CONGRESS CATALOGING-IN-PUBLICATION DATA

Kling, Andrew A., 1961-
  Surveillance / by Andrew A. Kling.
    p. cm. — (Crime scene investigations)
  Includes bibliographical references and index.
  ISBN 978-1-59018-991-7 (hardcover)
  1. Undercover operations—Juvenile literature. 2. Electronic surveillance--Juvenile literature. 3. Forensic sciences—Juvenile literature. I. Title.
  HV8080.U5K55 2008
  363.2'32—dc22   2007040390

ISBN-10: 1-59018-991-4

Printed in the United States of America
2 3 4 5 6 7 12 11 10 09 08

Contents

Foreword

The popularity of crime scene and investigative crime shows on television has come as a surprise to many who work in the field. The main surprise is the concept that crime scene analysts are the true crime solvers, when in truth, it takes dozens of people, doing many different jobs, to solve a crime. Often, the crime scene analyst's contribution is a small one. One Minnesota forensic scientist says that the public "has gotten the wrong idea. Because I work in a lab similar to the ones on CSI, people seem to think I'm solving crimes left and right—just me and my microscope. They don't believe me when I tell them that it's just the investigators that are solving crimes, not me."

Crime scene analysts do have an important role to play, however. Science has rapidly added a whole new dimension to gathering and assessing evidence. Modern crime labs can match a hair of a murder suspect to one found on a murder victim, for example, or recover a latent fingerprint from a threatening letter, or use a powerful microscope to match tool marks made during the wiring of an explosive device to a tool in a suspect's possession.

Probably the most exciting of the forensic scientist's tools is DNA analysis. DNA can be found in just one drop of blood, a dribble of saliva on a toothbrush, or even the residue from a fingerprint. Some DNA analysis techniques enable scientists to tell with certainty, for example, whether a drop of blood on a suspect's shirt is that of a murder victim.

While these exciting techniques are now an essential part of many investigations, they cannot solve crimes alone. "DNA doesn't come with a name and address on it," says the Minnesota forensic scientist. "It's great if you have someone in custody to match the sample to, but otherwise, it doesn't help.

That's the investigator's job. We can have all the great DNA evidence in the world, and without a suspect, it will just sit on a shelf. We've all seen cases with very little forensic evidence get solved by the resourcefulness of a detective."

While forensic specialists get the most media attention today, the work of detectives still forms the core of most criminal investigations. Their job, in many ways, has changed little over the years. Most cases are still solved through the persistence and determination of a criminal detective whose work may be anything but glamorous. Many cases require routine, even mind-numbing tasks. After the July 2005 bombings in London, for example, police officers sat in front of video players watching thousands of hours of closed-circuit television tape from security cameras throughout the city, and as a result were able to get the first images of the bombers.

The Lucent Books Crime Scene Investigations series explores the variety of ways crimes are solved. Titles cover particular crimes such as murder, specific cases such as the killing of three civil rights workers in Mississippi, or the role specialists such as medical examiners play in solving crimes. Each title in the series demonstrates the ways a crime may be solved, from the various applications of forensic science and technology to the reasoning of investigators. Sidebars examine both the limits and possibilities of the new technologies and present crime statistics, career information, and step-by-step explanations of scientific and legal processes.

The Crime Scene Investigations series strives to be both informative and realistic about how members of law enforcement—criminal investigators, forensic scientists, and others—solve crimes, for it is essential that student researchers understand that crime solving is rarely quick or easy. Many factors—from a detective's dogged pursuit of one tenuous lead to a suspect's careless mistakes to sheer luck to complex calculations computed in the lab—are all part of crime solving today.

Carlie's Disappearance

On the evening of Sunday, February 1, 2004, eleven-year-old Carlie Jane Brucia disappeared in Sarasota, Florida. She had spent the previous night at her friend's house on Bee Ridge Road, and around 6 p.m. she set off to walk home to her house on McIntosh Road, less than a mile (1.6km) away. She called her mother to say she was on her way. The walk should have taken fifteen or twenty minutes, but Carlie never made it home. When she hadn't arrived by 6:30 p.m., her stepfather drove around in his pickup for an hour and a half, looking for Carlie without success. He returned home, where he and Carlie's mother called 911.

The Manatee County Sheriff's Department, investigating Carlie's disappearance, retraced her likely route. They found that Evie's Car Wash, on Bee Ridge Road, lay between the two homes. It seemed possible that Carlie had taken a shortcut through the car wash property. The police discovered that the owner, Matt Evanoff, had installed motion-activated surveillance cameras for security. The following day, February 2, Evanoff gave the investigators access to his system. They discovered the cameras had recorded ten seconds of important footage.

It showed a dark-haired white male, with tattoos on his right arm and wearing what appeared to be blue mechanic's coveralls, approaching and speaking to a smaller white girl, who had come from the opposite direction. He talked to her for four seconds, grabbed her arm, and then led her away from the camera's field of vision, in the direction from which he had appeared. The time stamp on the video was 6:21 p.m., February 1. Carlie's mother and stepfather identified the girl in the video as their missing daughter.

The video evidence dramatically changed the course of the investigation. Investigators originally considered Carlie a potential runaway; now it was clear that she had been abducted. That same day, the sheriff's department released the video to the public, asking for any assistance in identifying the man in the video, and for help in finding Carlie. The surveillance video was broadcast not only in the Sarasota area, but throughout Florida and across the country as well. Hundreds of tips flowed into the police department, offering opinions about the man who was seen grabbing Carlie and pulling her

The surveillance video of Carlie Brucia's abduction by John Smith. This video led to Smith's conviction for murder.

away. Within two days, police had identified Joseph P. Smith, a thirty-nine-year-old mechanic who had lived in Sarasota for years, as a suspect. Smith was arrested and charged with her abduction, and, when her body was found, with her murder.

Carlie Brucia's abduction and murder made national headlines, in part because the abduction had been caught by a surveillance camera system. These systems have grown in both number and sophistication in recent years, and have contributed to crime-fighting and crime-solving efforts across the world. Skilled technicians use a variety of forensic science procedures to extract as much information as possible from the images obtained at the scene. But before they can assist their fellow investigators in determining what happened at a particular scene, they need to discover exactly what sort of information might be available, and to determine the best way of preserving, extracting, and studying the images captured by the surveillance cameras.

CHAPTER 1

"The Video Might Be Your Only Witness"

The arrest of Joseph P. Smith in connection with the suspected abduction of Carlie Brucia is one result of using surveillance video systems in crime scene investigations. Increasingly, across the United States, and in many countries abroad, law enforcement personnel take the same first step as Detective Steve Morgan of Kansas City, Missouri, Police Department: "One of the first things we do when we arrive at a crime scene is to look to see if there's cameras and try to look at that video. Then we look around the immediate area as well; other cameras might have picked up something that's related to the crime we're investigating."[1]

In some cases, the crime itself is caught by cameras installed at the location where the crime took place. In one instance, a camera caught a suspect crawling through a broken glass door in a restaurant, and recorded his movements as he reached across the counter to remove cash from a register and exited the way he came in. A series of cameras in a computer store documented the actions of an intruder who broke into the store in search of merchandise to steal, only to discover that every item was securely fastened to the display cases. A camera at a bank drive-through recorded the actions of two men as they put a chain around an automated teller machine, and then drove away, pulling it behind the vehicle.

In other circumstances, law enforcement investigators find video evidence from nearby businesses or landmarks that may help find suspects related to a particular incident. One of the

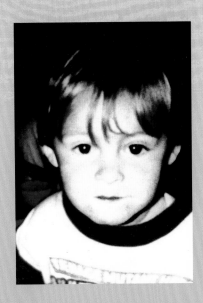

James Bulger, whose abduction from a London mall was captured on surveillance tape. Two ten-year-old boys were eventually arrested and convicted for Bulger's murder.

most famous cases occurred in Liverpool, England, in 1993. Detectives searching for two-year-old James Bulger, who had become separated from his mother in a shopping mall, discovered video footage of the toddler being led away from the mall by two youngsters, who were eventually convicted of murdering the two-year-old.

Since that time, the existence of surveillance video footage has grown into an asset that assists law enforcement on a daily basis. In May 2007, investigators in Florida arrested two suspects in an assault case, based partly on video evidence of the pair entering a convenience store before the attack occurred, and partly on their identification by the victim. A month earlier, detectives in Washington State solved the case of the November 2006 theft of a memorial statue to fallen soldiers and marines in Iraq. According to Chris Bristol, of the Yakima *Herald-Republic*, "While reviewing surveillance footage from the car wash, detectives spotted the statue in the bed of a pickup used by two men captured on tape prying open a coin box. The surveillance footage also captured the license plate of the truck."[2] Both of these cases would have been more difficult to solve without the presence of the video cameras.

Cameras in Daily Life

Surveillance cameras have become a common sight as we go about our daily routines. Banks install them at automated teller machines and behind the counters, looking over the tellers' shoulders. Retail outlets use them to record customers' movements throughout the store or activities in the parking lots. Cities position them above intersections to observe traffic patterns and to watch for accidents or vehicles running red lights. Schools install them to account for students and adults alike, to ensure the safety of both. Surveillance occurs at airports, train stations, bus stations, sporting events, race tracks, and casinos. We have become so accustomed to them that we may not even notice them.

According to technology writer, B. J. Goold, these "closed-circuit television" (or "CCTV") systems are simply "a number of video cameras connected in a closed circuit or loop, with the images produced being sent to a central television monitor or recorded."[3] The term "closed circuit" was originally used to differentiate between private networks of cameras and monitors and public television broadcasts, but today CCTV is used as a generic term to refer to a variety of surveillance camera technologies.

The Carlie Brucia case helps show the increasingly important role that such systems play in today's society. They can see and record events that might otherwise go unobserved, and can be an invaluable tool when it comes to investigating suspected or actual criminal activity. Thomas Christenberry, associate professor and director of the Digital Multimedia Evidence Processing Laboratory at the University of Indianapolis, and a retired investigator for the Federal Bureau of Investigation (FBI), sums it up this way: "In the absence of any human witness, the video might be your only witness."[4]

As recently as the 1980s, members of the business community had few choices of cameras and recording equipment when it came to surveillance systems. Similarly, members of the law enforcement community, when encountering a video surveillance system at a crime scene, recognized that the system likely consisted of equipment that had not changed substantially in design or technology for many years. Investigators would expect that the surveillance systems would likely consist of cameras and recording devices that were either part of "active" or "passive" monitoring.

By the Numbers

15

Average number of times per day a person is caught on camera in the United States.

A casino's security room. Most of today's casinos use "active" surveillance to monitor their gaming areas.

Active vs. Passive Surveillance

The two types of surveillance practices, "active" and "passive," represent two differing philosophies of security and information management. Each can be tailored to the needs of a particular facility or business, and each can provide vital information to crime scene investigators.

The history of active CCTV networks can be traced to World War II, when German engineers installed cameras at Test Stand VII at Peenemünde in 1942 to observe and study the launches of their V-2 rockets. Since that first installation, active systems have expanded far beyond rocket test launches. Today, as then, active systems require trained personnel to observe the on-camera events as they are recorded. These individuals use monitors to watch continuously the activities caught on camera. Current applications for active surveillance include casinos, banks, and airports. Observers watch the monitors for telltale signs of questionable activity, such as attempted fraud, attempted robberies, or attempted smuggling, and they assist crime scene investigators by pinpointing the specific moments when criminal actions occur or when suspects are observed.

On the other hand, passive surveillance systems record events without dedicated personnel watching the activity at all times. One or more cameras may be focused on the interior of a convenience store, or on various locations in an office building or factory, and these are connected to a recording device located somewhere in the building. Carlie Brucia's abduction at Evie's Car Wash in Sarasota was captured by a passive surveillance system that had started recording automatically when it sensed motion within its field of vision; even the owner had not known what was on the tape until he viewed it with the sheriff's department personnel. Although these systems do not have individuals watching the events being recorded, the footage they record can be an essential tool for investigators.

In real-life circumstances, according to Jerry Ratcliffe, associate professor of criminal justice at Temple University and a former law enforcement officer, many systems are a combi-

A Glimpse into the Future

One area of research that is being explored intends to mimic the human visual system, which allows human eyes to focus on one area but still be aware of what is going on beyond that specific location. At York University in Toronto, Ontario, Professor James Elder is developing a two-camera system that integrates the two types of vision used by humans.

To understand these two types of vision, imagine riding a bicycle. You can focus your attention on the road or on the trail ahead of you, but at the same time, you can detect when a dog runs up along side you. Your peripheral vision catches the dog approaching, and if you choose, you can focus on the dog or continue to focus on what is ahead. Elder's system mimics this ability.

One camera carries a wide-angle lens that provides a low-resolution view of an area, similar to peripheral vision, while the second has a narrower-focus lens that provides a high resolution view of a specific area. This camera is mounted on a motorized pan–tilt unit that allows it to change its field of vision based on different activity. For investigative purposes, according to Elder, "the system could make surveillance more efficient. It can, potentially, note unusual events, and register when they occurred, saving personnel the trouble of viewing many hours of video footage after a crime has taken place."

James Elder, quoted by Olena Wawryshyn, "York researcher improves video surveillance systems," *York University Y-File,* April 17, 2007. www.yorku.ca/yfile/archive/index. asp?Article=8248.

nation of both active and passive systems, "where recording devices record all images, and an operator scans from monitor to monitor, concentrating on some and ignoring others."[5] For some businesses or facilities, the operator may be an employee with no other duties. In smaller establishments, however, the operator may be an employee with many other duties, such as running a cash register.

Understandably, these other duties may make a crime scene investigation more challenging, as the employee may not have observed the activity on the monitor when it occurred. This forces the investigators to review the information captured by the system, in order to observe the action and identify the individuals involved. This information may have been captured by cameras in any number of locations throughout the business. After determining that a surveillance system is in place at a crime scene, investigators need to work with the system's owner to ensure that they are aware of the location of all cameras. Many will be immediately visible; others may not be apparent at all.

Overt, Semi-covert, and Covert

Law enforcement personnel arriving at a crime scene need to realize that the cameras they see upon their first inspection may not be the only ones in the area. A network's cameras can be divided into three types of visibility: overt, semi-covert, and covert. Overt surveillance makes up the largest part of commercial systems, with companies choosing to have their cameras fully visible to their customers and the public. These can be found at supermarkets and malls, and are often installed above doorways, within retail areas, and overlooking parking areas. They are often accompanied by signs that inform people that they are now entering an area under CCTV surveillance. In some cases, the cameras are connected to monitors that are also fully visible to the public, like the ones often seen at convenience stores.

Semi-covert systems are, by definition, less obvious to the public. They are popular in areas or businesses that wish to make it apparent that the area is under surveillance, but also wish to keep the coverage area a mystery. Investigators need to work closely with the system's owner to understand where

COMMUNITY
SAFETY

CCTV IN
OPERATION

020 7278 4444
6

CAMDEN

METROPOLITAN
POLICE

A sign in a London neighborhood alerting the public that the area is being monitored by CCTV.

its cameras are installed and its coverage area.

These semi-covert systems are often distinguished by small domes of one-way transparent plastic that hide the presence of the camera, and are particularly popular in areas such as airports and casinos. Investigators encountering these systems cannot assume that the criminal activity was recorded by the cameras behind the housings, because, according to Jerry Ratcliffe, one of the reasons this type of system appeals to businesses is that: "it also prevents the public from determining who is under surveillance and allows you to conceal the exact number of cameras in a system, as you are not required to install a camera in every casing."[6]

Covert systems have all cameras, hardware, wiring, and monitors installed in hidden locations. While some businesses or facilities will display signs that acknowledge the CCTV's presence, others may not. The main advantage of this configuration is that the cameras are not out in the open, and therefore are fairly immune to tampering or destruction. Also, if a sign is not posted, people will be unaware of their presence and may not be as careful with their actions.

Regardless of how the cameras are installed, a limitation of any system is the ability of the cameras to catch the action. As became apparent in the Carlie Brucia case, passive-system cameras can only record what is in their field of vision. The system did not record how long Joseph Smith had been near Evie's Car Wash, or where he took Carlie after they left the camera's field of vision. Personnel working with an active system may see more of a particular event by watching an adjacent camera's monitor. If the car wash's system had been monitored actively, Smith's activities before the abduction might have been recorded on an additional camera pointing in a different direction. Personnel might have captured Smith's vehicle on tape, and might have been able to alert law enforcement as the abduction was occurring.

This information might have been recorded by multiple cameras on multiple tapes, but evolving camera technology now enables systems to see much more than before. Originally, the only way you could change the direction in which the camera pointed was to adjust it by hand. Now, this adjustment and many others are available by remote control.

Professor Rama Chellappa has developed a video camera that will be able to detect potential problems without the use of human monitoring.

Pan, Tilt, Zoom, ..., and Observe

Active surveillance systems now feature cameras that can be remotely controlled. Personnel can direct the camera to "pan," or move laterally, on a pivot to follow the movements of a person or a vehicle. Other options mount the camera on a ball joint that allows the unit to tilt up and down as well as pan left and right. When mounted in the ceiling of a casino, for example, such options allow for a 360-degree range of movement to observe action throughout the room.

Such features require lenses that focus automatically, to ensure that the subject remains clearly visible. Additionally, some cameras have the ability to zoom in on a particular activity, for which automatic focus is also essential.

Intelligent Surveillance

At the University of Maryland, Professor Rema Chellappa and a team of graduate students have developed systems that connect a surveillance camera to the computer, enabling the camera to identify specific parameters of behavior.

In one demonstration of the system, Chellappa and his students set up two cameras and a laptop computer in a conference room. A student walked into the middle of the room, dropped a laptop case, and walked away. On the laptop screen, a green box appeared around the student as he moved into camera range, and another surrounded the case when it was dropped. After a few seconds, the box around the case turned red, triggering an alarm.

The camera recognized the normal appearance of the room's layout, but understood that the bag left unattended was an anomaly. The alarm notifies the system monitors that the bag needed to be investigated.

These functions mean that law enforcement personnel must investigate the field of coverage for each camera. Working closely with the monitoring personnel, they may discover important clues. Perhaps the crime itself was not caught by a camera, but another operator may have been panning across a room and in so doing captured a vital clue, such as a person of interest or a suspect before or after the crime.

At this time, the pan and zoom functions require a human operator to observe the action and to decide which control to activate. Current research, however, is working to develop software that may take part of the human element out the equation. For example, Professor Rema Chellappa and a group of students at the University of Maryland are developing systems that can recognize potential problems, such as unattended luggage at an airport, and can then alert surveillance personnel. This system could be used in both active and passive systems.

Both active and passive systems represent a significant investment of time and resources on the part of the businesses and organizations that purchase and use them, but they may prove to be invaluable to crime scene investigators. Any system requires regular maintenance to ensure its optimal performance, as well as personnel who understand the technology or, at a minimum, know how to keep the system running. For many employees involved with surveillance systems, this involves working with videotape cassettes that law enforcement personnel may require in order to investigate a crime.

Analog Video Recording

Many surveillance systems, like the one that caught Carlie Brucia's abduction, link cameras to videotape recorders (VTRs), which record the information on video cassette tapes, in the same way and with the same equipment that can record television broadcasts at home. This is known as "analog" recording, and, for the law enforcement personnel investigating Carlie Brucia's disappearance, the analog videotapes from the car wash were familiar technology.

In its most basic form, analog video recording is no different from the first moving pictures introduced more than one hundred years ago. Analog motion pictures are created by a series of photographs made in a high-speed sequence. Professor Christenberry says that analog recording works "like old-fashioned still cameras; the image, or signal, is imprinted directly on the camera's magnetic tape."[7] Alan C. Bovik, of the Department of Electrical and Computing Engineering at the University of Texas at Austin, likens analog recordings to "the signals and images that are abundantly available in the environment"[8] all around us.

With an analog system, the amount of information recorded and stored is limited by the type of recording device and the length of the videotape. Home VTR users are familiar with the different speeds of recording available; these varying speeds dictate how quickly the tape passes across the magnetic recording heads inside the tape machine. A standard setting records information at thirty frames per second; other settings can record as few as one frame per second and still capture enough detail for the action to be recognizable. Video cassette tapes come in standard and micro-cassette size, and vary in how much information they can store. Using long-running tapes and extended play recording settings, analog surveillance systems can record an entire business day on one cassette.

Many surveillance systems use videotapes similar to the ones that are used in homes to record television programs.

The investigators looking into Carlie's disappearance examined the analog tapes surrounding the time that they assumed she cut across the car wash's property. They quickly discovered the pictures of Smith leading her away from the scene. The analog images changed investigators' mindset immediately; they ceased making inquiries about a missing girl, who had perhaps run away from home, and began investigating a kidnapping.

Analog systems were once the only choice available for surveillance systems, and they remain a popular choice for many who wish to increase security inside and outside a facility. Detective Morgan states that as recently as 2004, analog systems comprised "as much as eighty percent"[9] of the installations that he encountered in Kansas City. Crime Scene Investigator Mitch Pilkington of the Sheriff's Department in Weber County, Utah, says that in 2004, between "ninety and ninety-five percent of what we saw was analog."[10]

These statistics meant that investigators had become accustomed to looking for videotapes when they encountered surveillance systems at a crime scene. However, advances in digital technology have created more choices in surveillance systems. Digital video recording has become more popular both professionally and at home, and is now becoming more widely used in security applications.

Digital Video Recording

In the same way that twentieth-century record albums recorded on vinyl were created in an analog format and compact disks are created in a digital format, digital video recordings consist of information that is, as described by Bovik, "converted into a computer-readable binary format consisting of logical 0s and 1s."[11] Digital and analog video recorders both use magnetic tape, but the difference between digital videotape and analog videotape is that the tape for digital recording is manufactured to accept a digital signal from the camera.

A further important difference between analog and digital video recording is how digital information is recorded on the tape. According to technology writer Scott Anderson, a timer looks at, or "samples," "the video stream 13.5 million times per second"[12] and converts it to a binary number. A single frame of

Digital video recorders, like the one pictured here, are being used more frequently by businesses as their main surveillance systems.

23

a standard full-color video picture would be 750,000 bytes, or 0.75 megabytes (MB), in size. The sheer size of the information recorded would make digital video impractical, because, according to Anderson, "multiply that by thirty frames per second and you get about twenty million bytes every second."[13]

Consequently, digital video signals are "compressed," or reduced in size, through a mathematical process called "discrete cosine transform." This process automatically scans the image, removing certain frequency ranges and storing the rest, and then restores the information when the images are replayed. The compression system reduces the information per second from 20 MB to about 3.5 MB, a ratio of approximately 6:1.

Advances in computer power and memory capacity have made digital video storage a practical alternative to analog systems. As faster and more powerful recording equipment becomes more affordable, digital systems are being used increasingly for everyday video surveillance operations. It is essential, however, that these systems, and particularly the videotapes on which the information is recorded, are managed in an efficient manner that will make them as useful as possible if they are needed in a crime scene investigation.

> **By the Numbers**
>
> ## 20
>
> **Megabytes (MB) of information in one second of uncompressed digital video.**

Maintaining the Videotape System

When law enforcement personnel arrive at a crime scene where videotaping was used, they hope to find evidence that will assist in their investigation. However, this may not be the case. The managers of the facility or business may not have understood the system's limitations, and may not have established a proper routine for storing, re-using, or recycling the videotapes that have information stored on them.

Christenberry says that his experience leads him to the

opinion that many small businesses will keep the tapes "about a month and then record over them."[14] Such recycling may seem sufficient for general use, but Sergeant Boyd Bryant, technology supervisor and public information officer for the Police Department of the City of Everett, Washington, says that this is not a proper way to maintain a system. During his almost thirty years on the job, he and his officers have visited businesses

> … where the entire tape is nothing but clear acetate because it has been used continuously for years. We also discovered that the metal oxides that made up the medium for recording would make solid bricks inside the recording mechanism as it ground away on the video recording heads.[15]

Eric Kumjian, a forensic analyst/robbery detective with the Miami Dade Police Department, agrees. His experience is that "a lot of the tapes are degraded because people don't know how to use the equipment, the lighting's bad, the camera angles are wrong or the magnetic tape itself has deteriorated."[16] These deficiencies can, at the very least, lead to delays in investigations, and, in some extreme cases, result in crimes going unsolved until such time as the criminal strikes again.

Crime scene investigators are, however, discovering that many businesses are choosing to eliminate the routines of storing, recycling, and re-using analog videotapes by removing the use of magnetic tape from the surveillance system altogether. This involves connecting digital video cameras to a computer for storage on a dedicated hard drive.

Digital Computer Storage

Individuals who have watched a video on the Internet, or have created a video with a cell phone, may be familiar with the concept of using a computer hard drive for video storage. Surveillance video techniques are similar; the digital video cameras are connected directly to a hard drive, and the images are available for playback on the same computer. Such systems are limited not by the length of a particular video cassette, but by the size of the hard drive.

Computer processor speeds and disk-drive storage capacities have increased greatly in recent years. Consumer desktop computers now come standard with the ability to play and create videos, thanks to multi-gigabyte hard drives that were unheard of just a few years ago. As a consequence, digital surveillance systems are becoming more and more popular. Their hard drives, often custom built for the business, are able to capture more hours of video with fewer compression concerns than older configurations. They remove the VTR from the operation, as well as the concern of storing and recycling videotapes. The only drawback, or limitation, is the size of the hard drive.

The growth of digital video surveillance may mean

This camera is connected directly to a computer hard drive. The advantage of using a computer for storage is that these systems are not limited by the length of a videotape, but by the size of the computer's hard drive.

additional convenience and security for business owners, but it also means additional challenges for crime scene investigators. Detective Morgan says he has seen a big jump in digital video use for surveillance systems in Kansas City. In 2004, they made up perhaps twenty percent of the systems he investigated; by 2007, that number was as much as forty percent.

As digital surveillance systems increase their share of the surveillance market, crime scene investigators need to keep up with the evolution of digital video analysis techniques. This includes the growing use of wireless networks and the Internet.

IP Video Surveillance

Increased connectivity through the World Wide Web, including broadband and satellite Internet access, has led to the development of wireless surveillance systems that use Internet Protocol (IP) technology. The system's cameras upload their images directly to an Internet server, and the images are viewed on a Web browser, and therefore can be viewed from beyond the confines of the business, with proper authorization. The information can also be recorded on a digital video recorder (DVR) for later playback and analysis. The advantages of this system lie in the ability to connect cameras wirelessly, and to take advantage of the superior storage capacity of IP hard drives. Additionally, the system can be established using older analog cameras that are already installed.

The attractive features of IP video surveillance have led to its installation in a variety of locations. According to market analysis company, Frost & Sullivan:

> The 6 million square-feet Wynn casino in Las Vegas is the single largest installation in terms of the number of IP cameras, in the last few years. When it takes shape, the new World Trade Center in New York too is expected to heavily utilize IP video surveillance.[17]

Car Cams

A police officer in Texas reviews a traffic stop he made earlier in the day on a digital camera system installed in his car.

Police departments across the United States started installing video cameras in their patrol vehicles in the late 1990s, partly in response to accusations of racial profiling during traffic stops. The original dashboard-mounted cameras were connected by cables to a videotape recorder (usually mounted in the vehicle's trunk) that recorded the information on 8mm or standard VHS tapes.

Since that time, these "car cams," and their records of traffic stops and vehicle chases, have been used in a variety of cases, and have appeared on television and throughout the Internet. Law enforcement agencies have worked with manufacturers to bring the car cam into the age of digital surveillance, thereby aiding the investigations of police-car-related incidents. Ohio State Highway Patrol officer, Robert Barrett, says, "the camera doesn't lie. I wouldn't trade it for the world."

The most advanced systems feature digital cameras that have the capability to stream video in real time to Web-based monitors at police stations, and are as small as 2.5 inches long by 2 inches high and 2 inches wide (6.35cm by 5.1cm by 5.1cm). These are mounted behind the driver's rearview mirror, and are connected to a computerized recording unit that records the action on a flash drive.

Robert Barrett quoted in John Futty, "Plan to equip Ohio police cruisers with cameras isn't in sight: Federal funding sought for costly devices," *Columbus Dispatch,* 2006. http://www.policeone.com/police-products/vehicle-equipment/in-car-video/articles/129845/

In some locations, these systems are being developed in conjunction with law enforcement personnel as a way of monitoring high-risk areas. For example, in the Chicago, Illinois, suburb of Bellwood, a security firm worked with the local government and police to install more than forty IP cameras that are monitored by the 911 dispatchers. This network augments an existing network of older analog cameras, and, since its development in mid-2005, the arrangement has benefited investigators. In one instance, the personnel discovered a midnight break-in in progress at a store across town. They dispatched investigators to the scene while the suspect, who turned out to be a wanted fugitive, was still inside.

Surveillance systems have changed significantly in the last decade, as advances in technology have added to the choices and options available to businesses and government agencies. They enable businesses to add an additional layer of security to their operations, and they continue to play an important role in the science of investigating crimes.

As the technologies evolve, crime scene investigators will be challenged by the growth and development of new surveillance techniques and equipment. This trend, however, is merely a continuation of the growth in surveillance video since the 1980s. During that time, analog video has virtually disappeared from the consumer market in favor of DVDs; eventually, it may also disappear in commercial security settings. Digital video on cassette tape may also some day be replaced by Internet-server-based storage. Until that time, the technologies associated with both analog and digital surveillance will remain in use.

The impact of these evolving technologies continues to affect forensic video analysts on a daily basis. Not only will these crime scene investigators need to understand the concepts associated with both the older and evolving technologies; they will also need to remain proficient in the techniques of analyzing information from older systems, while also mastering techniques for working with newer systems. No matter

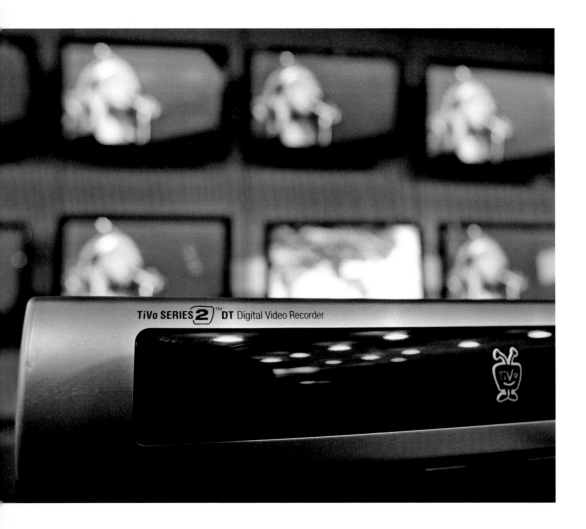

Surveillance video can be saved on a digital video recorder, such as this, to be played back and analyzed at a later date.

what sort of surveillance video network they encounter, their task will continue to be to extract as much information as possible from the equipment and the technology they encounter at each crime scene, in order to bring their investigations to a successful conclusion.

CHAPTER 2

Collecting the Evidence

Law enforcement personnel arriving at a crime scene have a great many responsibilities, such as securing the scene from further disturbance to protect evidence, and safeguarding the witnesses and victims. Additionally, they assess the location and the surrounding area for surveillance cameras, a practice that has become more widespread in the past few years. As Lieutenant Brian McNulty of the Haines City, Florida, Police Department puts it, "like the old cliché, a picture tells a thousand words. A video tells, how many? A million?"[18]

Once the investigators determine that video surveillance was in use at the scene or at adjacent locations, and that they need to view what the cameras may have caught, they need to discover where the recording equipment of the various systems is located. This may involve dealing with multiple cameras from several businesses or agencies, as well as with different system technologies.

A business using an analog system, such as a small shop or convenience store, will likely have the equipment in a location that is easily accessible. A facility using a digital system with IP storage may present greater challenges for investigators. Additionally, the evolution of digital video surveillance has led to a wide variety of system manufacturers and equipment types that may restrict access to the recorded information. Consequently, the investigator, or forensic video analyst, must approach each situation with care in order to not only

By the Numbers

40%
Percentage of American police vehicles with some sort of in-car video.

Cell Phones at the Scene

*A*growing trend in technology is the use of cell phones to create videos of crime scenes. For example, in January 2007, a cabinet minister from the Nova Scotia government was forced to resign following the broadcast of a cell phone video that showed him leaving the scene of an accident. The video was made by a witness at the scene and was sent to the media. Videos made by subway riders during the 2005 London Underground bombings were also broadcast throughout the media.

Recognizing this trend, crime scene investigators now look not only for surveillance cameras but for cell phones that were present at or near the scene of the incident. Law enforcement personnel ask crime scene witnesses or individuals in the immediate area for permission to examine their phones. The hope is that vital clues in the crime's investigation may exist within the images that were being created at the time.

Crime scene investigators now look not only for surveillance cameras, but also for cell phones present at a scene that may have captured important evidence.

Not only have cell phone videos been created during a crime, but some have even been created by the criminals themselves. According to Crime Scene Investigator Mitch Pilkington, of Weber County, Utah, Sheriff's Department, a new fad among criminals is to "make videos of themselves while they're committing the crime, and they can't believe it when we seize their phone and find them on it."

Telephone interview, Crime Scene Investigator Mitch Pilkington, April 23, 2007.

respect the property of the owner, but also to ensure the integrity of the information on the system.

Gaining Access

In many cases, gaining access to the surveillance system is as easy as following cables. Many overt systems, such as are found at convenience stores, have wiring that investigators can follow from the camera to a monitor that is located in plain sight, such as behind a cash register. The VTR is often located under a counter or in an adjacent storeroom. If the system is analog, gaining access to the surveillance information generally is as straightforward as turning off the tape machine and removing the tape.

Analog tape used in surveillance situations is almost exclusively in the VHS format; other formats have disappeared from the consumer market. For example, one convenience store case investigated by Kansas City's Detective Morgan involved a VHS system. The system's cameras caught a gunman who "held the counter person at gunpoint, got the money, and then shot him anyway and escaped."[19] Retrieving the information from the system in this case was simply a matter of removing the tape for examination.

Retrieving digital information is more complicated, as the system often involves information recorded on a DVR or on a hard drive. The Law Enforcement and Emergency Services Video Association (LEVA), a nonprofit video training association, has created a guide for forensic professionals that addresses the rapidly evolving field of digital recording. The guide was developed by leading video forensic practitioners, and is used by law enforcement individuals and organizations throughout North America. The guide offers suggested standard operating procedures for investigating such systems

> ### By the Numbers
>
> **$4 MILLION**
> **Estimated cost to outfit 300 Kansas City, Missouri, Police Department patrol cars with digital in-car camera systems.**

and for retrieving "digital multimedia evidence," or DME.

The guide lists a variety of barriers that may restrict immediate access to the system. For example, the forensic video analyst "should coordinate with personnel at the storage location to gain access to secured areas, locked containers, or storage devices . . . . Additional security barriers, such as password protection to the host computer and to the DVR viewer, may need to be overcome."[20] The guide also recommends that the investigators note the make and model number of all recording equipment, as well as take photographs of the equipment in place before they conduct any work with it. This practice will ensure an accurate record of their activity in the event that their role in the investigation is reviewed by their organization or in conjunction with a trial. With the documentation in place, the analyst can move on to preserving the pertinent DME that exists on the system.

Many overt surveillance systems, like the one that was used to capture this robbery at a convenience store, are located in plain sight.

In some cases, a forensic video examiner must extract a computer's hard drive, as was done here, in order to obtain a piece of video evidence.

Preserving the Data

Preserving the analog or digital multimedia evidence is an important step within the crime scene investigation. Law enforcement personnel need to take precautions to ensure that pertinent data is not destroyed or overwritten during their activities. As Christenberry points out, this is more of a problem with digital systems than with analog tapes. With analog videotapes, information that has had other information recorded over it "is often recoverable during the analysis,"[21] but with digital recording, such information is basically destroyed during the re-recording process.

Consequently, with any digital system, the investigators must ensure that the relevant data remains intact and is not overwritten. The best way to prevent data loss is to power down the system according to manufacturer's recommendations. LEVA's guide points out that simply unplugging the digital video recorder (DVR) is not recommended; as many personal computer users have discovered, a sudden loss of power can lead to loss of data.

DVRs will keep the information in their memory for a certain period of time, and then overwrite it with new data, but that period of time varies by manufacturer. The investigators need to determine what will be done with the original information that remains on the system. LEVA counsels that leaving the DME on the system could make it susceptible to later tampering by non-law-enforcement personnel. The group recommends that the question of "whether to erase or not to erase is best left to agency policy, but should be considered in each case."[22] Regardless of the decision, the guide reminds the analysts that the situation must be fully documented in their notes.

After ensuring that the data will not be overwritten before it can be studied, the investigator next needs to determine the best method for extracting the evidence. When Detective Morgan investigated a shooting at a dance club on a night when the club was supposed to be closed, he needed to review what the cameras recorded. After examining the system, he felt he had three options available for extracting the DME. His first option was to try to determine who had installed the system, as "sometimes the company puts a sticker with their name on the computer,"[23] and contact them to extract the information. Secondly, he could have the police department's computer forensics staff called to the scene. Lastly, he could determine if he could copy the desired information onto a DVD directly at the scene.

Each of Detective Morgan's choices applied only if the DME is stored at the scene of the investigation. Some businesses, such as banks with multiple branches throughout a city or region, now choose to have their surveillance information pooled in one off-site location. Gaining access to this type of data can be more challenging.

Off-site Storage Access

Obtaining access to data that is stored in a physical location away from the crime scene may be impractical. The forensic video analysts and the law enforcement investigators need to find out exactly where the stored data is located. In these circumstances, the LEVA guide counsels that "if physical access is not practical, the [analyst] may elect to contact other

Becoming a Forensic Video Analyst

Job Description:
A forensic video analyst's duties include performing technical darkroom photographic and digital work; creating and enhancing digital photo images; and utilizing video technology and other techniques to identify suspects. A forensic video analyst also assists in reviewing, analyzing and processing evidence materials and exhibits for court and investigation purposes, prepares and maintains a variety of records, works closely with a variety of contacts, and attends court as required.

Education:
A bachelor's degree from a four-year college is often required, with possible majors including law enforcement, photography, or computer software.

Qualifications:
A forensic video analyst must have some related experience, preferably in a law enforcement environment, and have completed courses in video production, editing and analysis, photography, digital imaging and enhancement, and related computer software.

Additional Information:
Currently, there are few licensing and certification requirements for forensic video analysts, as the occupation is one which is still evolving. Groups such as the Law Enforcement & Emergency Video Services Association (LEVA) and the International Association for Investigation (IAI) are comprised of individuals who work to establish training standards and to develop universal best practices.

Salary: $40,000 to more than $75,000 a year.

A forensic video analyst must arrive at a crime scene prepared with equipment, such as a laptop and adapters, in order to analyze surveillance video as quickly as possible.

personnel who can access the DME and make arrangements to preserve the data."[24]

Crime Scene Investigator Mitch Pilkington of Weber County, Utah, Sheriff's Department, has had several cases involving off-site data storage. He says that retrieving such data first means contacting the company that has the information, and then explaining exactly what information is needed. The process can be time-consuming,

especially when you're dealing with a case like a bank robbery. It may take a couple of days [for the information to arrive]. The company may send it as an e-mail, or as a DVD, or sometimes they send the wrong clip—it's not what you're looking for—and you have to start all over again.[25]

The main advantage, he says, to having access to the information on-site is that it allows him to make the best choices possible concerning what he retrieves. For example, a particular camera angle may present more (or less) information that originally thought. By inspecting the entire DME on-site, he can choose to copy only what he feels will be the most useful at that point, which is particularly important if time is of the essence in the investigation.

For both Detective Morgan and CSI Pilkington, the severity of their cases makes data retrieval all the more urgent. Unfortunately, discovering where the data exists is only part of the challenge facing the investigators. Once the storage location is found, the next step is creating a connection between the storage system and the analyst's computer.

Connectivity Issues

Just as there is a wide variety of ways to connect personal computers to other devices, such as printers, personal data assistants, cell phones, external hard drives, and music players, there is a variety of interconnect devices available for the forensic video analyst. The LEVA guide counsels that the analyst needs to be familiar with a variety of connection technologies. These include USB, Firewire, parallel and Ethernet cabling, as well as connections to CD and DVD drives.

The analyst needs to inspect the storage device, and determine the best way to connect it to his equipment, which may include a laptop computer or a separate hard drive. He or she needs to come prepared with a variety of connection options, as well as different adapters. For example, most laptop computers include "ports," which enable connections to other equipment or computers, but not all ports are the same. For example, some ports have nine connecting pins, while others have twenty-five. Consequently, the well-prepared analyst will arrive at the scene with an adapter that can connect a twenty-five-pin cable to a nine-pin port.

Connection complications arise if the DME is stored at a remote site. The analyst will need to determine what options are best for retrieving the data. It may be possible for the investigator to retrieve the data using the system's network connection, or via a telephone cable.

Examining these options, and determining the best method for retrieving the DME from an off-site storage facility, also raises the question of legal authority. The jurisdiction in the place where the data is stored may have different laws governing data. It is possible that employees of the business where the crime has occurred may not have the legal authority to allow access to and retrieval of the information. A warrant may be necessary before the investigators are allowed to connect to the system.

When the challenges of storage location, connectivity, and legal access have been addressed, the investigators can now turn their attention to the information itself. The next challenges in retrieving DME are often posed by the particular equipment involved in the recording process.

Incompatible File Formats and Equipment

Forensic video analysts discover that they need to be familiar with a wide variety of DVRs that are used in the surveillance market. In the best-case scenario, the analyst uses his or her experience to identify the software that the recorder uses to create the DME. Some manufacturers use software that may record the information in any one of several types of common file formats. The information can then be played back in "open source" video players, such as QuickTime or Windows Media

Player. These recognize several types of file formats, such as files with the suffix .wma or .mpeg. The analyst needs to determine if the DVR's data can be read and played back with these open-source applications before any DME is retrieved from the system.

In other cases, the DVR manufacturer may use a non-standard file format that can only be played back by its own brand of video players. The analyst must determine if additional software is needed to read and play the DME on an open-source player, or if the DVR's system can convert the files into a more common file format for the analyst's use. These variations in file formats has led LEVA to admit that "because many DVR systems capture, transmit, store and playback video data in unique ways, a single forensic approach for the acquisition and examination of digital video evidence does not exist."[26] This undoubtedly puts pressure on the investigators to retrieve the evidence intact.

Additional variations in DVR recording and playback occur in the compression and decompression techniques used by

Lossy compression used in digital video recording is the same compression format used for the popular mp3 file format used in many portable music devices like the Ipod.

the manufacturers to make the size of the digital information files manageable. These methods, called "codecs" (which is an abbreviation of "compression and decompression") will greatly affect the way in which the digital information is saved.

The Role of Codecs

Codecs lie at the heart of making digital video recording, storage, and playback practical. These systems use mathematical algorithms to encode and decode the data, and they determine how the information will be managed. In order to store the large amounts of data of a digital video on a computer hard drive, most codecs employ "lossy" compression technology.

Lossy compression changes the nature of the original

Tape Reconstruction

Forensic video analysts do not always have the benefit of finding surveillance data intact. For example, a case in Missouri involved a convenience-store robber, who grabbed the store's videotape and cut it to pieces. Cassettes can get dropped, smashed, and otherwise damaged—accidentally or on purpose—and part of the analyst's job is to recover as much information as possible from the tapes, regardless of their condition.

LEVA's training course titled "Advanced Forensic Video Analysis and the Law" includes an exercise that puts reconstructive skills to the test. On the third day of the five-day class, the participants, who come from law enforcement agencies around the world, gather in a parking lot. There, large trucks run over videotape cassettes, completely crushing them. The students then have to pick up their pieces and reconstruct the tape into a new cassette case, with their goal being to retrieve as many usable images from it as possible.

recording, whether it is digital video or digital audio. With digital audio, an uncompressed music file, such as are found on commercial CDs, can be several megabytes in size. The popular mp3 file format, used in many portable music devices, uses lossy compression to reduce the file size for a player with a smaller memory capacity, but it also reduces and eliminates some of the music file's information. The difference in sound quality between the uncompressed and the compressed files is usually unnoticeable. But with video files, lossy compression can reduce or eliminate vital details and accuracy within the picture.

For example, surveillance footage from an ATM camera that captures a vehicle's license plate may, after lossy compression, lead to an inaccurate interpretation of the plate's numbers; an eight may look like a zero or the letter E may look like the letter F. It is, therefore, essential that the investigator understand basic codec functions and how they will affect the DME in the player.

CSI Pilkington has had his share of run-ins with unknown codecs. Occasionally, he encounters a video that he cannot view with an open-source player, due to the system's particular codec. "You can only watch that video on that particular machine, or with their particular software,"[27] he says, adding that the variety of players, codecs, and networks in digital video present obstacles that were not present with analog systems.

After the issues associated with access, connectivity, and format have been analyzed and addressed, the forensic video analysts can now move on to retrieving the DME from the system. Once again, however, the lack of one standard format hinders the data retrieval process, and the investigators must determine the best method on a case-by-case basis.

Retrieval Challenges

Retrieving surveillance video that has captured a crime in progress can be essential in an investigation. Unfortunately, the presence of cameras and a surveillance system at a scene does not guarantee that law enforcement personnel will be able to retrieve useful footage. The cameras may not be actual working devices (in other words, they have been installed to give the impression that the area is in under surveillance), or the cameras may have been pointed improperly, so that the action did not appear on them. In other cases, as CSI Pilkington says, the video simply doesn't exist, "because of a system malfunction or because the system didn't start recording"[28] when scheduled.

Occasionally, investigators discover that the system contains useful information, but that they are unable to remove the videotape from the recording device. In one such circumstance, Detective Bill Coakley, of the Woburn, Massachusetts Police Department, recounted that he used a portable recording sys-

Investigators may find that some DVR have a function that allows data files to be exported onto a recordable DVD.

tem to retrieve the information, saying, "I brought the system to the store, hooked it up, and found the images I was looking for, and recorded them off their equipment. That was it."[29]

This method is also possible when investigators encounter a digital recording system. Although LEVA cautions that this "always results in degradation of the image,"[30] because an analog copy of a digital image reduces the clarity of the images, the footage may still be useful. Other options, which are generally more preferable, are possible, and will result in a better copy of the DME.

Other Retrieval Options

The key to retrieving the video images needed for the investigation sometimes lies within the system itself. Some DVRs automatically make a backup of their DME files, so that the law enforcement personnel may only need to find and manually copy these files, leaving the original files intact. The key to copying backup files is ensuring that all other files that might be relevant to the event are also copied. These include the media player's information, including the company that developed it and its version, and files that contain important information about the recording, such as the time and date that it was created.

Investigators may also find features within the DVR's programming functions that may aid data retrieval. During his investigation of the dance club shooting, Detective Morgan discovered that the club's DVR had an option within the record function that allowed data files to be exported. After halting any further recording, he exported the pertinent information onto a recordable DVD. Within a matter of minutes, he had the data he wanted for the investigation.

Another possible feature allows the user to freeze the video and capture a single image in a separate file. CSI Pilkington likens this "capture still" action to the methods that allow personal computer users to print the information displayed

Steps in a Process: Comparing the "Working Copy" to the Original

An essential duty of a forensic video analyst is to ensure that the digital surveillance video that will be subjected to scrutiny during the crime-scene investigation is as complete a record as possible. To ensure the accuracy of this "working copy," it must be compared to the original digital video record. This will help verify that the best evidence has been extracted, and it will offer a means for verifying if any changes have occurred.

1 The original digital media evidence (DME) is placed in one digital video recorder (DVR). The working copy is placed in another DVR. The two records are played simultaneously.

2 The analyst checks the DMEs for "artifacts" (visual aberrations) within the records. If an artifact is present when viewing the original DME, the same artifacts should be present in the working copy.

3 If the artifacts are different in the extracted files, the analyst should determine the cause. Some possible explanations may be:
   (a) conflict between software versions (being viewed on a different version than that on which it was recorded)
   (b) differences in the display viewing technology (such as computer monitors)
   (c) differences in color settings or sample frequencies that can result in the same video having a different appearance when viewed on different computers.

4 The software being used to view the video can cause changes to the color information, resolution, or aspect ratio of the DME. For example, DME that is viewable using Windows Media Player may have a different aspect ratio and some shifting in color values when viewed using a QuickTime viewer.

on their monitor's screen, or to capture the screen shot as a separate image file. While this particular option captures only individual pieces of a larger video, and, of course, does not capture the motion aspect of the video, it may be the only way available to retrieve the desired information.

A final option, which may be a last resort, requires investigators to seize the recording system. CSI Pilkington agrees that all other options should be investigated before having to remove the system. "I'd hate to put [the system's owner] at further risk,"[31] he says, pointing out that such action will leave the location without its security system for an unknown period of time while technicians try to remove the DME.

When the DME has been preserved and extracted, the investigators need to compare the copied files, called a "working copy," with the originals. This process serves as verification that the copied information is an exact duplicate of the original, or is as an exact copy as possible.

Verifying the Working Copy's DME

The variety of video players and codecs means that simply copying the files from the DVR or the hard drive may not be enough to ensure that the working copy contains the most accurate information possible. There are several reasons why the investigator must play the working copy alongside the original data for a visual comparison.

For example, many DVRs change the nature of the video images, so that they can be played on an open-source player. The data gets recompressed to another file format, and this invariably results in some loss of detail in the working copy. Viewing the footage side by side provides the opportunity to ensure that the working copy is an accurate reproduction of the original.

One of the visual checks the analyst makes is for speckles or blocks in the footage, called "artifacts." These visual imperfections in video recordings are often due to the technical limitations of the camera. For example, a camera that is recording an area of bright sunlight will often generate artifacts, as its lens cannot accommodate the amount of light. The analyst must look closely to ensure that any artifacts present in the working copy are present in the original.

Some cameras can produce images that seem stretched or flattened in comparison with actual objects. This results from an altered "aspect ratio," which is the relationship between the height and the width of an object. For example, objects may appear wider and shorter, or taller and skinnier, than they are in real life. Checking the working copy's aspect ratio assures the analyst that objects or individuals that are 6 feet (1.8m) tall in actuality will be represented accurately by the working copy.

After the analyst has verified that the working copy represents the best possible duplication of the original DME, he or she can begin to investigate the content of the working copy for clues to solving the crime. In some cases, the crime's forensic video analysis will consist of working with only one video; in other cases, it may include multiple videos from multiple systems from multiple locations.

Time is often of the essence in forensic video analysis. Some cases will, unfortunately, fall victim to the law enforcement department's hierarchy of important cases. These will await analysis until the investigator has time available, being set aside because more pressing cases require immediate examination. Regardless of when the analysis begins, the key remains the same: extracting useful information that will assist in the investigation and prosecution of the crime caught by the surveillance cameras.

CHAPTER 3

Forensic Video Analysis

The Web site for the Metropolitan Police Service of London, England, contains a page with a gentle warning to owners of video surveillance systems. The police encourage owners to ensure that their systems are working properly and are maintained regularly. The page includes a very grainy photo of an individual; the photo quality is so poor that it is impossible to tell much about the person. The text says that the photo "is an example of what can happen when things go wrong. If the CCTV system that recorded this image had been correctly adjusted and properly maintained then it could have provided vital information"[32] that would have helped apprehend the individual.

The use of video surveillance in Great Britain, especially in the nation's cities and, specifically, in London, far exceeds its use in the United States and Canada. The Metropolitan Police have been using it to help investigate crimes for many years. Two notable cases are the 1999 nail-bomb attacks in the Brixton neighborhood of south London, when they analyzed more than 25,000 hours of footage, and the London subway bombings of 2005, when they combed through 20,000 CCTV tapes during the investigation.

Such high-profile and long-term investigations are the exception rather than the rule in the field of forensic video analysis. A few, such as Carlie Brucia's disappearance, hold the public's attention for days, until there is some resolution, or

> **By the Numbers**
>
> # 300
> **Average number of times per day a person is caught on camera in London, England.**

until another headline grabs more air time. The vast majority, however, involve local crimes that may make local headlines for a few days and then fade from the public eye until some new development comes to light. In more and more cases, a new development is the result of a study of one or more sets of surveillance footage, and the development may lead to a significant break in the case.

It is this behind-the-scenes work that often goes unnoticed by the public, yet it is as painstaking as any other forensic discipline. Brett Hallgren, of the Vancouver, British Columbia, Police Department, sums up his role this way: "Our primary mandate is the proper extraction of evidence off of the videotape for presentation in the courtroom."[33]

Part of the key to any forensic investigation is having the right equipment. Law enforcement agencies and their personnel need to make effective decisions based on several factors when buying equipment. The equipment needs to be cost-effective and appropriate for the tasks, and needs to be based on research on what works best for each agency. Consequently, there are many different ways in which different agencies accomplish the tasks.

By the Numbers

500,000

Estimated number of surveillance cameras in London, England, including systems on buses and trains.

In the Field or in the Lab

As computers have increased in speed and memory capacities, they have played an increasingly large role in forensic video analysis. For some investigators, the best way to take advantage of this is with custom-built computers for the lab. Others prefer being able to take their work with them to the crime scene.

CSI Pilkington works in Weber County, Utah, north of Salt Lake City. He prefers to have his video processing equipment in the lab. He says his choice was based on his

jurisdictional area. "I can be anywhere in our county, or be back to my lab, in twenty minutes,"[34] which, he believes is a close enough distance to be able to begin to process any video in a timely fashion, even on priority cases.

His lab features a desktop computer that was custom-built for his video work. He notes that it also needed to meet department specifications for security. For example, he says that to help safeguard his work, it does not connect to the World Wide Web, which could make his system or the department's network vulnerable to hacking.

On the other hand, Investigator Scott Slavin, of the Seminole County, Florida, Sheriff's Office, feels that the best use of his time is to be able to take video processing equipment with him in the field. He feels that this allows him to have the tools to begin analyzing the surveillance video at the crime scene. He chooses to use processing software on high-end laptop computers, which supplement the equipment in his lab.

Regardless of where the investigators choose to begin their analysis, their equipment needs to meet the evolving demands

Law enforcement officials need to make effective decisions, based on several factors, when purchasing equipment that will be used to analyze video evidence.

Steps in a Process: Preparing a Surveillance Video for Analysis

Investigators use a variety of equipment to analyze surveillance videos. Many companies provide computer programs and equipment, but the process is similar regardless of the software and hardware used.

1 A videotape is placed in a videotape recorder (VTR), which is connected via a video capture card to a computer hard drive.

2 With the VTR power on, the analyst turns on the computer and starts the video analysis program. The program opens a "preview" window.

3 The analyst starts the video playback in the VTR. The footage appears in the preview window in a digitized format.

4 When the tape reaches the section related to the investigation, the analyst begins copying the information to the hard drive through the program's "capture" option while the tape continues to play. Most analysts will copy information both before and after the section of interest to ensure accuracy and to avoid repeated playback of the actual tape (to minimize potential damage).

5 The software saves the footage on the hard drive for later analysis.

of their field. Although digital video systems are increasing in number, the majority of surveillance systems still use analog-based recording. Forensic video analysts have a wide variety of tools and techniques at their disposal in order to extract usable evidence from these tapes, and a key to the direction the analyst takes is the way in which the footage was recorded.

Multiple Speeds, Multiple Images

In standard analog video operations, information is recorded on a videotape at thirty frames per second. This speed is sufficient for recording a film from an over-the-air television broadcast; a standard tape purchased at a store will generally allow for two hours of recording at a standard speed. Consumer VTRs generally have other recording speeds available, with some allowing up to six or eight hours of recording on one tape. This slows the recording rate to significantly lower than thirty frames a second (the rate varies with manufacturer and speed). Consequently, the quality of the video is significantly decreased along with the rate of recording.

In order to allow for a full-day's-worth of surveillance information, many VTRs connected to surveillance cameras will record information at an even slower rate to place more information on a single tape. According to videographer, Jay Gelber, the slower rates "vary by manufacturer, and can be as slow as one or two frames per second for very slow speed recordings."[35] In addition, many systems will use "multiplexing," in which one VTR is connected to as many as thirty-two high-speed cameras.

Multiplexing comes in three different forms. In "quad-screen," information from each camera is recorded on one quarter of the film's frame. Other systems, using more cameras, will record each camera's information on a single frame consecutively. In this method, camera one's information goes on the first frame, camera two's on the second frame, and so on until each camera has captured one frame of data and the process returns to camera one. The third type of multiplexing uses "interlacing," which takes advantage of how television information is created. Standard television in North America uses 480 horizontal lines of information to create a screen image; interlacing puts one camera's image information on the even-numbered lines and the second camera's information on the odd-numbered lines.

A tape with both video recorded at a slow frame rate and multiplexing presents the forensic video analyst with a variety of challenges. Detective Morgan recalled a convenience store robbery, which was caught on several cameras both inside and outside the store. He explained that the tape recorded both the incident inside the store, and also an altercation between the suspect and the store's clerk outside, in the parking lot. "The clerk had given [the suspect] the money, but then followed him outside and confronted him, and the guy shot him."[36] The incident took place at night, and the footage of the outside shooting was poorly-lit. In this case, the Kansas City Police took the VHS tape and began to examine it frame by frame.

Frame by Frame

One way to examine a videotape with time-lapse photography is to run it through a machine called a digital frame synchronizer. Jay Gelber uses one to assist the Fairbanks, Alaska, Police Department with CCTV images, and he explains that the system allows him to "speed up or slow down the tape. First, I play the tape at its regular speed—the speed it was recorded at—and then I can speed up and slow down the playback until I get a normal speed."[37] From there, he can proceed through the video to examine it frame by frame for the information the police require. When he finds a frame that he feels is useful, he halts the playback. The synchronizer then enables him to make a digital image of the frame, which he then transfers to his computer for enhancement.

The frozen images, or "stills," that are captured by the synchronizer are, according CSI Pilkington, essential to any crime scene investigation. They are among the best pieces of

This combination of frame by frame images shows a mentally disabled man being attacked with a baseball bat. The frame by frame method is a useful way to exam a videotape.

evidence an analyst can add to the process. Unfortunately, the chosen stills may not capture as much information as the investigation needs. Some details will be lost if the subject of the image, such as a person or a vehicle, is in motion. After creating the stills, the analyst will then try to enhance the images as much as possible.

Digital image technology allows for a great number of enhancements. Many basic imaging programs on personal computers will allow the home user to modify digital photos. Users can remove flash-created "red-eye" or alter the color balance and the luminance (or brightness levels). However, as with any digital image, there is a point at which the stills from the surveillance videos cannot be improved any further.

To demonstrate this, Jay Gelber opens a file in his computer of an individual facing the camera, standing at a counter inside a room. The photo is grainy, but the individual is definitely male, and his skin color is fairly discernible. The room appears to be the interior of a bank, with the individual at a teller's window. Gelber says that the Fairbanks police provided him with a videotape in conjunction with an investigation. He captured this still from it, and enhanced the image into what was on the screen.

Gelber notes that this image may not be nearly as helpful as it may seem at first. Although the image may lead an investigator to reach conclusions about the individual and the setting, Gelber says that he'd rate it about a three on a scale of one to ten. Gelber points out,

> How tall is he? How much does he weigh? What color is his shirt? Is it white or yellow? Is he African American or Hispanic?
>
> Is he really standing inside a bank? What's going on behind him?
>
> We can't tell from this image. There's just not enough information there.[38]

Working with similar videos, CSI Pilkington applies a process called "frame averaging." He describes the procedure as similar to working with layers in the popular digital imaging program, Adobe Photoshop. He creates a number of stills from frames that feature the same subject, such as a suspect's face or a parked car. These frames are usually, but not always, adjacent to each other in sequence on the videotape, so occasionally he will choose a frame from another part of the video for the operation. He then adds the images together, one on top of another in successive layers. Frame averaging "helps to sharpen the details as much as we can, but it only works if the object's not in motion. Otherwise, it's not much use."[39]

Frame Averaging Leads to an Arrest

In January 2003, police in Columbus, Ohio, made an arrest in connection with a series of rapes that had occurred on and around the Ohio State University campus. The assaults had begun in May 2002, and were followed by fraudulent use of the victims' credit or debit cards at local ATMs. It was analysis of surveillance video from one of the ATMs that led to a vital clue that helped break the case.

One of the victim's bank cards was used after dark at a local ATM. Video footage from the ATM's camera was almost completely black, except for a pair of car tail lights. Josh Hodson, the forensic video specialist for the Ohio Attorney General's Office, used frame averaging to lighten the footage enough to reveal the vehicle's license plate number.

That information led them to the suspect, who was put under close observation by Columbus police. He was confronted by undercover officers in nearby Dublin, Ohio, as he tried to use another stolen credit card at another ATM. He led the officers on a foot chase before being apprehended. He was first charged with possession of stolen property, but subsequent evidence connected him to the rapes and a variety of other associated felonies.

Frame averaging requires a certain amount of image quality for it to succeed. Working with full-frame video is best, says CSI Pilkington, but unfortunately many of today's videos are multiplexed, and the quality of the individual images within each frame will vary from camera to camera within the particular CCTV network.

De-multiplexing

The main benefit of a multiplexed system is that the owner is able to create videotape records of more locations within a business than with a standard, single-camera system. Reviewing the information on the VTR on which it was recorded will yield multiple images on the monitor arranged like tiles, with each picture presenting the action caught by its particular camera. Unfortunately, playing back that same video footage on any machine other than the one on which it was recorded will give a distorted and unclear record of the action. According to Shelli Hisey, a criminalist with the Arapahoe County, Colorado, Sheriff's Office, "When you look at a multiplex video [on a normal VTR], you just [get] a series of flashing images and you can't really see any type of story take place."[40]

For the forensic video analyst, de-multiplexing used to be more than a challenge; it was an extremely tedious chore. Detective Bill Coakley, of Woburn, Massachusetts, described working with multiplexed tapes as frustrating. "We had a lot of tapes we couldn't do anything with. We just couldn't break a lot of them down [for analysis]."[41] CSI Pilkington recalls that with such a tape, he had to run the video frame by frame, and capturing stills took hour after hour of exacting and monotonous work. However, advances in software have allowed analysts like Pilkington, Coakley, and Hisey to complete tasks in a fraction of the earlier time.

New computer programs can perform both frame averaging and de-multiplexing automatically, and allow analysts to make much better use of their time. CSI Pilkington recalled that it allowed him to slash dramatically preparation and stills

development time on a recent video associated with a homicide investigation. He said that what would have taken him two weeks to perform manually now takes about two hours. For Criminalist Hisey, the advanced software encouraged her to analyze the multiplexed video from an assault case investigation. The case had become stalled without further information, and she recalled that the new system "allowed me to isolate camera views in order to watch the [assault] take place in real time and in sequence."[42]

There comes a point, however, when the analysts find that, given their equipment and expertise, they cannot extract any more information from a particular video. At this point, when the images can no longer be enhanced, law enforcement agencies often choose to turn to other forensic video analysts. With the video of the bank interior, the Fairbanks police decided to enlist the aid of the Federal Bureau of Investigation (FBI) by sending the footage to one of their computer labs for further analysis.

A video analyst de-multiplexing a videotape. Once a tedious chore, new computer software has cut considerably the time it takes to de-multiplex video evidence.

Assistance from the FBI

For many years, the FBI performed its video analysis at one facility in the Washington, DC area. For example, the FBI assisted the Manatee County Sheriff's Department by enhancing the video of Carlie Brucia's abduction. Their efforts yielded a clearer image of the man's shirt, his tattoos, and the apparent name tag on his shirt. The enhancements allowed the analysts to estimate the abductor's height at 5 feet 8 inches (1.73m).

U.S. Attorney for the North District of Texas and a FBI special agent analyze some video evidence at the North Texas Regional Computer Forensic Laboratory. Today, there are fourteen of these labs throughout the United States.

Other instances of federal and local cooperation led the FBI to assess its entire computer forensics program. As the number of law enforcement cases involving surveillance video grew, and as the requests for federal assistance increased as well, the FBI increased its assistance capabilities.

Beginning in 2002, the FBI started to expand its assistance to law enforcement agencies in cases concerning computer forensics, including video analysis. Today, there are fourteen "Regional Computer Forensic Labs" across the United States. At these centers, FBI employees and law enforcement personnel on assignment from nearby agencies work with videos from a variety of sources. Some videos are sent in from law enforcement agencies that do not have the equipment or personnel necessary for forensic examinations. Others are sent in from agencies hoping that the labs can extract more information than they could.

At the Regional Computer Forensic Lab (RCFL) in Kansas City, Melissa Hamley of the FBI works on a variety of videotapes in all sorts of condition. Some are damaged, and others have been erased, either deliberately or accidentally. Hamley runs through them, frame by frame, looking for clues that will aid an investigation.

In an interview with the Kansas City Star newspaper, Hamley said one of the most common procedures at the lab is to freeze video frames in order to generate stills with better detail than the original investigating agency could generate. For one case, she succeeded in taking a series of images that were, for all intents and purposes, completely black, and lightened them enough to yield a car and its license plate.

The advanced technology and the expertise of the individuals at the RCFLs enable them to work with video from various agencies and extract information that ordinarily might go undiscovered. Presently, their work consists mostly of analog videotapes, but the move to digital systems is changing the field of forensic video analysis.

Becoming a Criminalist

Job Description:

A criminalist's duties include, but are not limited to, collecting evidence at crime scenes as well as performing and/or supervising the analysis of samples collected as evidence, such as hairs, fibers, fingerprints, tool marks, videotapes, and other types of forensic trace evidence required in scientific criminal investigations.

Education:

A bachelor's degree from a four-year college is required with a major in criminalistics, chemistry, biology, or physics. This usually includes successful completion of eight semester units of general chemistry and three semester units of quantitative analysis. Some crime labs require a master's degree in forensic science or criminalistics.

Qualifications:

There are no licensing and certification requirements for criminalists. Crime labs are accredited by a national accreditation association and city, county, and State labs conduct regular proficiency tests of their criminalists.

Additional Information:

In addition to scientific expertise, a criminalist must also have good information gathering and organization skills, critical thinking skills, and the ability to communicate orally and in writing.

Salary:

$30,000 to more than $65,000 a year.

An Overland Park, Kansas, police officer shows surveillance video of a moving truck used to abduct a teenager. If a person or object is in motion within an analog video, this section of the tape may appear blurry when the tape is stopped.

The Challenge of Digital Video Forensics

For many businesses, moving to a digital surveillance system is based on economics. A digital system, particularly one that stores information on a hard drive or on an IP-based server, represents more modern technology than an analog system connected to a VTR. CSI Pilkington understands why analog systems are being replaced; he says a digital system has fewer moving parts, and is less time-consuming for the business's staff. "A [software installation] 'wizard' guides them through the installation on their computer, and they can set up an automatic schedule for when the system records,"[43] so they no longer have to program the VTR. Additionally, part of the appeal of a digital system is the prospect of no longer having to change and store videotapes.

The move to digital, however, presents increasing challenges for video analysts. Grant Fredericks, a former law enforcement officer who now performs video analysis consulting and serves as an instructor for LEVA, has analyzed thousands of hours of video over the years. He has definite opinions about

Fake or Altered Videos

The Internet has become the storehouse for many photo-based pranks and hoaxes. The image of a shark leaping from the water toward a helicopter was widely shown before it was proven to be actually two unrelated pictures merged together. Now, a professor at Dartmouth University wonders if videos will be the targets of such manipulations.

Professor Hany Farid and the Dartmouth Image Science Group are working to develop software tools that will allow investigators to detect video that has been altered, either intentionally or unintentionally. Farid has created similar tools for investigating digital photographs, based on the ways that particular cameras and imaging programs capture data, and has provided expert witness testimony in a case concerning a series of stills from a surveillance camera. The defense contended that the evidence had been significantly altered by the police. Farid demonstrated that, although the police had run the images through Adobe Photoshop, based on the digital signature left behind by the program, it did not appear to him that they had significantly altered the evidence in the process.

His new work is more challenging. It has led him to the conclusion that video is difficult to alter with the current technology, and "the tools to tamper with video are not as sophisticated as those for photos, but we might as well get a jump on it."

Hany Farid, quoted in Michael Kanellos, "Are fake videos next?" CNET News.com, September 11, 2006. http://news.com.com/Are+fake+videos+next/2100-1008_3-6113449.html.

working with digital video.

> It's ironic that, by digitally compressing video to save it on hard disks, the digital video security industry ends up discarding information that is vital to forensic video analysis. Add the lack of standards that currently exist in digital video recording to the fact that people are building video servers in their garages and basements, and one can understand why digital video is fraught with problems for the average CSI.[44]

Professor Christenberry points out that, unlike analog tape, from which a previous series of images can be retrieved after re-recording, "once you've recorded over with digital video, the original information is pretty much gone." CSI Pilkington says that with basic digital systems, the quality of the information recorded by the camera is often less than that of a comparable analog camera. Detective Morgan adds, "with digital video, the camera might be able to pan and zoom, but with the image that's captured, that's pretty much all there is."[45]

One other essential difference between digital and analog recording is that analog uses distinct frames that can be observed by slowing and halting the video. Videographers, and others who work with digital video, will refer to frames within the footage, but this is actually a carryover from the days of analog. When an analog video is halted, the screen will display a complete image. It may include blurry sections, if a person or an object was in motion within the video. However, when a digital video is halted, what often appears is a collection of pixels that appear to have been spattered across the screen, which may not yield a discernible image with which the analyst can work.

All of these circumstances mean that one single forensic approach for the examination of digital video evidence does not exist. Therefore, the analysts increasingly need to rely on their own motivation to keep their knowledge current, and on their expertise to keep their work accurate. Fortunately, the move to digital is being accompanied by innovations in forensic technology as well.

Working with Industry

As video technology continues to change, and the field of forensic video analysis continues to adapt to those changes, companies that developed systems for analyzing analog tapes have added tools to enable the analysis of digital information as well. They receive feedback from field personnel, independent consultants like Fredericks, and from organizations such as LEVA and the International Association for Identification, the members of which perform fingerprint, tire tread, and forensic video analyses around the world.

This practice of cooperation, feedback, and development has resulted in a number of advances in the last few years. Manufacturers now offer systems with a wide range of forensic video tools that enable the investigators to capture, process, and output digital video evidence without altering the DME. These systems can de-multiplex digital signals, or allow the analyst to highlight individuals within the video, which the system will then follow throughout the footage. Others allow investigators to process cell phone video information. Some companies market portable systems that investigators can connect to surveillance systems; others enable their programs to be installed on existing laptop computers.

Both industry and forensic video analysts benefit from these cooperative efforts. The companies benefit from working in partnership with customers, who know what they need from the products, and the video analysts benefit from having the tools they need to perform their jobs more effectively. In addition, the law enforcement community as a whole benefits from this partnership, as effective forensic video analysis often contributes a great deal to the teamwork that result in the successful investigation and prosecution of crimes.

CHAPTER 4

A Team Effort

In almost every crime scene investigation, the forensic video investigator is part of a team that assists in the pursuit of clues and suspects. Sometimes, the law enforcement agency is a small group of individuals who perform many tasks, including working with surveillance videos. In larger jurisdictions, police departments may have a dedicated team that concentrates their efforts solely on forensic analysis of computers, photographs, and videos. In all cases, the individual who examines the surveillance video for clues works with others inside the agency (and sometimes with other agencies as well) in the pursuit of clues, victims, witnesses, and suspects. It is this team effort that brings results.

From the initial report of the crime, through its investigation, to its eventual resolution, the forensic video examiners work hand-in-hand with patrol officers, detectives, and other members of their law enforcement agency. They provide regular updates on the progress of the investigation, feedback on the video analysis, and completed products, such as isolated video clips and stills. In addition, they receive feedback from the other members of the team, such as witness statements, which can assist their efforts as they examine the videos.

Working as part of a team also requires the analysts to understand the priorities of the cases involved. Some will always be a higher priority than others, and these cases demand the immediate attention of all involved. A murder case, with which video may be associated, will take precedence over a case such as a home invasion or vandalism. The best investigators understand that certain projects will need to be put aside in favor of more pressing matters.

Priority Cases

The first indication of a new case's potential priority comes with the call-out. When law enforcement personnel are dispatched to a scene, they quickly assess what other resources will be needed. For Detective Morgan, the shooting inside the dance club demanded his immediate attention. Two men had been shot; one had died at the scene, and the other was in the hospital, severely wounded. He needed to examine the surveillance video as soon as possible. After reviewing the DME, he discovered the crime had been caught on camera. Viewing the video at the scene yielded no clues as to who had shot the victims, as the gunmen had been facing away from the camera the entire time. Detective Morgan decided to re-examine the video at the police station to see what else he could discover.

For CSI Pilkington, the call-out gives him the location and the crime, but few of the details about what he might discover and what evidence he might need to process. Arriving at a bank robbery, for example, he says he will process the scene immediately for time-sensitive items such as fingerprints and notes, and move to surveillance video at the direction of the investigating personnel on the scene: "In a priority case like a robbery, I'll begin to

Time-sensitive material, such as fingerprints, are often processed at a crime scene before investigators move on to analyzing surveillance video.

examine the video on the spot, and watch it with the detectives and the FBI to see which angles or sequences are important, and to determine which stills could be valuable."[46] With the important clues identified, he can return to his lab to generate the clips or stills that were requested, in order to keep the investigation moving.

Criminalist Hisey worked with her department's detectives to re-examine the video of the assault case from the previous year. The attempted homicide had begun as a fight in a bar, and escalated into a stabbing. The detectives had identified who had been in the bar when the stabbing occurred, but contradictory statements from witnesses and suspects had led to a deadlock. Using her newly acquired software, Hisey was able to isolate key pieces of evidence from the multiplexed video, including scenes of the assault from two different camera angles, which she then provided to the detectives for their use in the investigation. For these detectives, these video clips provided a key piece to the bar fight puzzle. Armed with this new evidence, they returned to their notes and began to re-interview persons of interest.

By the Numbers

$3.8 BILLION
Amount spent on video surveillance systems worldwide in 2005.

"The Defendant Was in That Melee"

During the initial investigation of the bar stabbing, some of the bar's patrons identified a particular individual as the perpetrator. The man denied he had committed the crime, and accused one of his friends, who had also been in the bar. The friend, in turn, denied it had been him. The detectives had arrested the suspected individual but were unable to make any further headway until Hisey's new analysis arrived in their hands. She noted that: "what the videotape showed was the fact that the friend that was being accused of doing the stabbing was not in the middle of the melee [fight] . . . that was occurring at the time. But you could see that the defendant was in that melee."[47]

Detective Morgan's investigation of the nighttime shooting of the convenience store clerk had a similar break. When the video was enhanced, his team was able to identify a car that was in the parking lot at the time of the incident. The case remained pending at the time of the author's interview, so the detective was not at liberty to go into many details of the investigation. He was, however, able to comment that the identification of the car in video, in conjunction with other information, gave a valuable clue that is being used in the investigation.

In both Morgan's and Hisey's cases, videos have been used in conjunction with other key evidence, such as eyewitness testimony. In other cases, such evidence may not exist, and investigators may turn to outside help for further assistance with their case.

Calling on the Experts

As the acceptance of forensic evidence has become more widespread in criminal justice, there has also been a rise in specialized fields within the realm of forensic analysis. Disciplines such as forensic odontology (the study of bite marks and human teeth characteristics) and forensic entomology (the study of insects in and around human remains) were relatively unknown until the last decades of the twentieth century. Along with these people are individuals who specialize in forensic image analysis, whose expertise can provide a more thorough interpretation of a video's content.

One technique the experts use is called photogrammetry. According to the Scientific Working Group on Imaging Technology (SWGIT), it is "most commonly used to extract dimensional information from images, such as the height of

By the Numbers

FEWER THAN 700
Number of forensic video experts in law enforcement agencies across the United States in 2006, according to the International Association of Chiefs of Police.

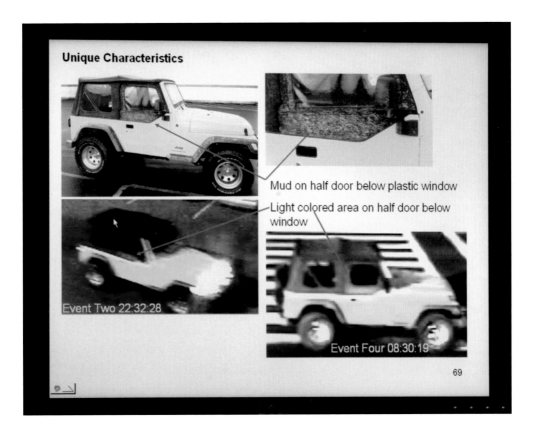

Unique Characteristics

Mud on half door below plastic window

Light colored area on half door below window

Event Two 22:32:28

Event Four 08:30:19

69

subjects depicted in surveillance images."[48] For example, the forensic image analyst may examine a still of a bank robbery, in which eyewitness accounts are lacking or unreliable, to reveal some important clues. Given the known measurements of physical features within the video, such as the bank teller's counter, and some advanced geometry, the analyst can determine the height of the suspected bank robber.

Additional forensic image analysis includes the study and comparison of facial features that are, for the most part, unalterable. A criminal, wishing to deflect suspicion, may change his or her hair color or style, or even have plastic surgery to alter the nose. Despite such changes, many features, such as the individual's ear shape and pattern, will likely remain unaltered. A comparison study of video stills can help match potential suspects, even if one video shows an individual with long,

A forensic imaging expert used these surveillance images to compare unique characteristics of a suspect's Jeep. The suspect was on trial for murdering his father.

Surveillance Video Databases

All individuals have physical or behavioral features that are unique to each person. These include a person's signature, voice, fingerprints, DNA, and facial characteristics.

Two screen shots showing individuals captured in a facial recognition surveillance video database. The database uses software to capture facial features and then converts the data into searchable information.

Computers are now being developed with facial recognition technology that turns measurements of individual faces into data for later comparison. New software that works with IP-based surveillance systems is being developed that, in the future, may make use of facial recognition technology to anticipate crime instead of just observing and recording it. The system is designed to receive a feed from a surveillance video system, and then use the software to capture an individual's face, and extract facial recognition data such as shapes and size of ears, nose, and eyes. It will then convert the data into searchable information.

In the meantime, the International Association of Chiefs of Police has opened three forensic video labs, and plans to open a fourth, in the United States. At these labs, analysts are searching thousands of hours of surveillance videos to extract information such as clothing, type of weapon, or type of business targeted. Their goal is to have these centers create a national database for law enforcement agencies, so that investigators can search video evidence for commonalities between their cases and others nationwide.

blonde hair and the other shows one with short, red hair.

Some cases may involve experts from fields unrelated to photography or video. An expert on physiology can lend advice to the study of individuals in a video by studying their stride or their posture, to determine if an individual seen entering a facility in one set of clothing is the same one who exits wearing a different set. A graphologist may be enlisted to study an individual's handwriting as it appears on a video. By watching as the person signs a visitor log or fills out a bank slip, the expert can determine if persons of interest are using the same grip or have similar writing characteristics.

Additional experts may aid the investigation. A surveillance video or a still may not give the investigators a sufficient view of an individual's face for their purposes, which may lead the investigators to call on a member of the agency with more artistic skills.

Forensic Artists

Some cases may require the involvement of an artist in the investigation. A law enforcement agency may enlist the aid of a forensic artist to create a three-dimensional representation of a suspect, based on a partial view of the person, such as when the individual only appears in profile on the video. This model representation can then be used in flyers and other publications seeking information about the suspect. The artist may also assist, for example, in the preliminary identification of a hostage victim seen on a video, by estimating the person's height and weight.

Since the end of the twentieth century, scientists have worked to develop ways of generating these representations using computer applications. An emerging field of three-dimensional graphic representations is allowing researchers to make additional use of stills created from surveillance videos. The computer measures various features of the individual's face from the still, and creates a three-dimensional, full-face simulation. Additional research may allow such representa-

A forensic artistic standing with a model he created. Law enforcement agencies sometimes call upon forensic artists to create three-dimensional models of a suspect when the surveillance video is not clear enough to give a good view of the person.

tions to be developed from video footage, rather than relying on stills.

These simulations and representations have a wide variety of uses within the law enforcement community. They can be used in missing persons posters, on wanted posters, or for inter-agency alerts. They may also aid investigators when working with witnesses.

However, in some circumstances, the investigating agency will decide to reach beyond the law enforcement community by enlisting the aid of the general public. The investigators may determine that they need the public's help in identifying individuals related to the crime. They may choose to release stills or clips from the video, or, in some cases, the entire video itself.

Going Public

The decision to release information from a crime scene surveillance video is not always an easy one. As Detective Morgan puts it, the agency has to weigh the consequences and the benefits involved. "If the release of the video is going to endanger the lives of the witnesses, we definitely won't do it,"[49] he says. CSI Pilkington adds, "is the quality of the video good enough that releasing it is going to help?"[50]

In the case of Carlie Brucia's abduction, the Manatee County Sheriff's Department decided that releasing the video was not likely to harm any witnesses, as no other individuals appeared in it, besides Carlie and her abductor, and that the quality was clear enough that someone might recognize her abductor. Their decision turned out to be the correct one. By the end of February 2, 2004, the day the video was released to the public, the sheriff's department had received eight hundred tips.

Crime writer David Krajicek summarized the calls:

"'The person's name is Joe Smith,' said one tipster, a friend who said he recognized Smith from the haircut and his gait. A second 'stated emphatically that (the) guy on video was definitely Joe Smith.' A third, a woman, said she was '100 percent sure (the) suspect is Joe Smith.'"[51] Smith was arrested the following day.

Since then, countless other videos have been released to the public. Although CSI Pilkington says that in his experience, the number of those released is truly a small percentage of those that related to an investigation, there are many that catch the attention of the local and national media. For example, a surveillance video clip from inside an apartment building in New York City was aired in early 2007, showing an individual mugging a woman, who turned out to be 101 years old. After a similar mugging and robbery of an 85-year-old woman, the New York Police Department distributed the video to every officer in the city and assigned dozens of detectives to the case. Police later made an arrest and charged a suspect, based in part on the tips generated by the widespread distribution of the video.

Joseph Smith being escorted to court by bailiffs. Smith was convicted of Carlie Brucia's abduction and murder based on the use of surveillance video.

For Detective Morgan, the decision to release the surveillance video of the dance club shooting was based on the case's urgency. One of the victims had survived the shooting, but, while in the hospital, he was unable to communicate. Rather than release a clip that showed the shooting, Morgan's department released a portion of the video from before the incident. It showed two women, who left before the shooting occurred, talking to the suspects. Morgan's team hoped that releasing the video would encourage the women to come forward, and that the women could help police identify the shooters.

After the video was released to the media, the two women did came forward and identified the two men in the video who were suspected of the shooting. The police arrested the men, a pair of brothers, the following day. As of writing this, the suspects remain in custody awaiting trial.

In other cases, however, releasing a video has turned up no leads at all. This has been the case of Dr. David Cornbleet, a Chicago dermatologist, who was found murdered in his office in October 2006. Surveillance video from the building caught an individual entering the lobby, walking down a corridor towards the doctor's office, and exiting the building as well, all at about the time the police feel the doctor was killed. Although the video was released to the public, the killer remains at large as of this writing.

The release of the Chicago surveillance video is one example of the increasingly interconnected nature of twenty-first-century society. Although the Chicago Police Department said that the killer had left substantial forensic information at the scene, which would take time to analyze, they wished to get the video out to as many people as possible, as quickly as possible. To do so, they used the Internet.

Internet Surfers on the Team

More and more personal computers are connected to the Internet through high-speed connections that allow their users to listen to streaming broadcasts, to download purchased music, and to watch videos. Many newspapers and television stations have their own Web sites, and will post video clips of news stories on them for viewers to watch at their leisure.

For many years, law enforcement agencies have sent surveillance video clips to the media for broadcast purposes, and many of those videos appear on the Internet. For example, Internet surfers can find the video of Carlie Brucia's abduction on several sites. The Chicago Police Department released the surveillance video of the person of interest in Dr. Cornbleet's murder to local media outlets for them to post on their sites. In addition, other videos of more local concern can be found on television station sites across the continent, as law enforcement officials work with the media to enlist the public's assistance.

Examples of this partnership grow daily. During just the first week of May 2007, law enforcement agencies released a variety of videos to the media, including the following: In Bakersfield, California, KGET broadcast and posted a video of a hit-and-run incident that killed a young girl. KRQE of Albuquerque, New Mexico, covered a story that involved a surveillance video capturing a possible suspect in a rape case. A robbery at a video store in Kansas City, Missouri, was captured on video, and was posted on KMBC's Web site. The Web site for WTVJ in Miami, Florida, displayed surveillance video of an armored car heist.

Although such sites are accessible worldwide, most are of purely regional interest, except when covering national or international events. Recognizing this, some law enforcement agencies have turned to other types of Web sites for video distribution. YouTube.com has millions of people accessing its site on a daily basis, and it has become an additional outlet for law enforcement agencies wishing to further an investigation.

"This is the First Time . . . Police have Utilized Video Web Posting"

In November 2006, a stabbing occurred in the parking lot of a Hamilton, Ontario, dance club after a hip-hop concert. Two men were stabbed, one fatally. Most of the concert-goers were in their late teens and early twenties, so the police department decided to upload the video of patrons arriving at the concert to YouTube.com. They hoped a site visitor would recognize their person of interest. Hamilton police posted a one-minute, twelve-second clip from the surveillance footage, and their efforts were rewarded when an individual turned himself in.

Staff Sergeant Jorge Lasso told a press conference, "this is the first time Hamilton police have utilized video web posting in an investigation, and to the best of its knowledge, the first time that law enforcement has ever used it as a direct investigative tool."[52] Following the success of the Hamilton Police Department's use of YouTube, Chicago Police and Dr. Cornbleet's family created a profile on the popular social networking site MySpace.com. The profile includes clips from the surveillance video, how to contact the Chicago Police, and reward information.

It also helped clear an individual who had been observed in an earlier video at a Home Depot outlet. The man had purchased an item similar to one found at the scene of

Dr. Cornbleet's murder, and after voluntarily meeting with the police, he was cleared of any further suspicion. However, after many thousands of hits and continued expressions of support from visitors to the site, Dr. Cornbleet's killer remains at large.

Enlisting the assistance of Internet sites is valuable and useful, especially if it helps law enforcement agencies with their investigations. However, it is only one resource available to them, and during the case of two missing children in March 2007, a team effort used a wide variety of resources during the case, including surveillance video.

Amber Alerts, the Internet, and Surveillance Videos

The 2007 disappearance of Remi and Lars Baugher did not capture the nation's attention in the way that Carlie Brucia's

Police agencies have begun posting surveillance videos on popular Internet sights, such as YouTub. com, with the hopes of receiving tips on unsolved cases.

did. However, it gained a good deal of publicity in the Pacific Northwest, and eventually involved authorities from the states of Washington, Idaho, Montana, Wyoming, and Colorado, and the FBI.

After the children's father failed to return them following a court-supervised visit in Walla Walla, Washington, family members alerted local police. Law enforcement in Washington State and the FBI issued an "Amber Alert" for the children

Remi and Lars Baugher

On March 25, 2007, an Amber Alert was issued in the state of Washington for two missing children. John Baugher was believed to have abducted his children, Remi, four-years-old, and Lars, two, from their home in Walla Walla. On the morning of March 27, the FBI alerted police in Missoula County, Montana, that Baugher had used an ATM near the Missoula airport. Reports of sightings of Baugher and the children that morning led investigators to check surveillance video footage from nearby businesses.

They discovered two important pieces of evidence. One video showed Baugher, an unidentified woman, and the children at a fast food restaurant. The other caught Baugher, carrying Remi as Lars walked behind, entering a clothing store less than two miles from the restaurant.

The Missoula videos gave authorities a starting point. Further sightings and tips were prompted by the release of the videos and by the Amber Alert. Baugher was arrested on March 29, near Denver, Colorado, as he tried to take the children to Salt Lake City, Utah. The children were unharmed. Baugher was charged with two counts of custodial interference in the first degree (a felony), along with one count of violating a protection order and one count of contempt of court. He was placed under house arrest in April 2007 pending a trial.

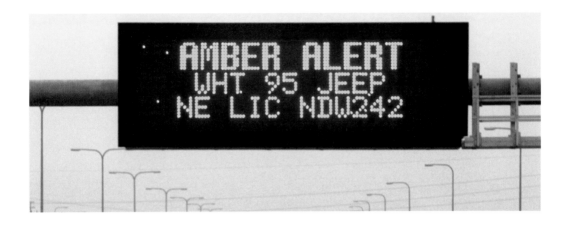

An Amber Alert posted on a Nebraska freeway. Amber Alerts are a way for law enforcement agencies to notify the public about suspected child abductions.

and their father. An Amber Alert is a way for law enforcement agencies to issue special notifications concerning the suspected abduction of children. Similar in principle to a severe weather alert, an Amber Alert goes out to media outlets, and may often appear as text alerts on highway traffic signs. In addition, they are issued as cell phone text messages and are posted on a variety of Internet sites.

In the case of the Baugher children, the alert gained coverage in Missoula, Montana, where citizens believed they saw the children and their father two days after their disappearance. Local officials investigated the sightings, and found important surveillance footage of the children. The videos provided valuable information, suggesting that Baugher had tried to change Remi's appearance by cutting and dyeing her hair. The videos were released to the public later that day, and were instrumental in the children's recovery.

The Amber Alert system is not without its critics. One of the criteria for issuing an Amber Alert is a suspicion that the missing child has been abducted, and many point to the Carlie Brucia case as one of its shortcomings in its present form. Because the Manatee County Sheriff's Department did not originally believe that Carlie had been abducted (they first considered her a runaway), they did not issue an Amber Alert until Monday evening, February 2, after they had viewed the surveillance footage from Evie's Car Wash.

It became clear in the following few days that by the time the Amber Alert was issued, Smith had already sexually assaulted and killed Carlie. Critics of the alert system in its present form point out that it was the surveillance video's broadcast, and not the Amber Alert, that led authorities to Joseph P. Smith.

In retrospect, authorities were extremely lucky in the Carlie Brucia case. Without the surveillance video, they would have not understood that she had been abducted. Without the video, they would not have received hundreds of tips pointing them to Smith. They were also fortunate in that Smith did not decide to leave the area or the state, with or without Carlie. Law enforcement officials nationwide now consider such actions as a possibility in many cases, and disseminate surveillance video clips, stills, and information throughout the law enforcement community.

Keeping a Lookout Across Agency Lines

Law enforcement agencies understand that, as with many members of today's society, criminals may move from place to place. As CSI Pilkington puts it, "crooks are mobile now, too,"[53] and investigators work to combat the possibility of perpetrators succeeding at the same crime in different areas. They also understand that criminals may return to the scene of the crime for further activity if they feel they have succeeded the first time.

The key to both situations is information. Some law enforcement agencies cooperate across jurisdictional lines to improve communications. For example, detectives from several departments in northern Utah meet monthly to discuss and update cases. This includes studying surveillance video stills as part of their "be on the lookout" routines. Other agencies have an in-house newsletter that includes summaries of cases

Becoming a Detective

Job Description:

A detective investigates crimes, interviews witnesses, victims, and suspects. He or she directs activities at crime scenes, including obtaining clues and preserving evidence; records progress of investigations; and aids police officers in the apprehension of suspects or offenders. He or she serves as liaison between his/her department and other bureaus, units, or departments at the local, state, and federal level. A detective also assists in the preparation of cases for court, and obtains depositions for assigned cases.

Education:

Education requirements vary by agency. Some require a college degree with a criminal justice major; others require a high school diploma only.

Qualifications:

On-the-job experience in law enforcement, a minimum of three to five years, preferably in patrol duties or sheriff's deputy duties. Some departments require that this experience is gained within the particular department or state.

Additional Information:

Work is generally supervised by a lieutenant or a chief of police, but detectives often have wide latitude for actions and judgment. Excellent physical condition may be a requirement of employment. Continuing education in criminal justice, as well as skill in vehicle use and firearms use, is usually required.

Salary:

$36,000 to more than $90,000 per year.

for all to read; the Nashville, Tennessee, Metropolitan Police Department's newsletter features narrations of interesting cases from across the city.

The March 2007 edition of this newsletter included an example of a successful team effort between the city's school department and the Nashville Police. A series of burglaries at a Nashville elementary school was solved thanks to the presence of surveillance cameras, and the success of inter-agency cooperation:

> The break in the case came when McGavock High School Resource Officers Mark Wells and Mitchell Burgess noticed a car in the high school's parking lot that very closely resembled a vehicle recorded by a surveillance system during one of the burglaries. That car belonged to a 16-year-old McGavock 11th grader . . . . He was interviewed by Detectives Jeff Ball and Ricky Stewart and admitted to taking part in the burglaries. [Two other teens were interviewed and also arrested.] Stashed inside the home [of one of the teens] and in a backyard tree house were the fruits of the burglaries, including computer equipment, stereo equipment, and a variety of sports equipment.[54]

The charges facing the teens included several counts of burglary and vandalism, and might never have been brought without the presence of the surveillance video.

For the crime scene investigators, the team efforts that accompany any investigation in which video plays a part does not end when a person of interest is brought in for an interview or when a suspect is arrested. The video analysts continue to work with agency personnel, as well as local, state, or federal prosecuting attorneys, until the case is declared closed.

CHAPTER 5

Evidence All Can Understand

More and more in today's society, surveillance video evidence is contributing to police case work around the globe. Investigators look for its presence when they arrive at a crime scene. They work with skilled technicians to extract what may be essential information from the surveillance system, and work with other members of the law enforcement community to examine the data for vital clues. What they find may make or break a case.

The footage from these cameras may evoke an emotional response. Few who have seen the haunting footage from Evie's Car Wash of the abduction of Carlie Brucia will forget it. The images of the suspect in Dr. David Cornbleet's murder, walking deliberately through the building, as if he knew exactly where the cameras were placed, are frustrating; Dr. Cornbleet's family wonders exactly how long the individual had been planning the murder.

Other clips may provoke rage or sympathy, or both. But the investigators pursuing the case need to remain objective, keeping in mind that, in the United States, anyone accused of a crime is innocent until found guilty in a court of law. Investigators may look at surveillance video footage and believe that they know the individuals in the pictures, but that instinctive reaction alone is not enough for a conviction.

The forensic video analysts also need to ensure that whatever actions they take to extract information from the footage is thoroughly documented. This includes making detailed notes throughout the process of analyzing the data, as well as writing complete reports when the analysis is finished. To that end, all forensic video analysts must have a command of the written word, so that anyone who reads the report will be able to understand it.

Command of the Written Word

Many members of law enforcement agencies look at writing reports as tedious or boring. They may believe that it interferes with performing their patrols or other police work, but they understand that these reports form the backbone of any investigation. They understand that, in order to document effectively their part in a crime scene investigation, their reports need to be clear and concise.

By the Numbers

4 BILLION

Hours of video per week generated by surveillance cameras.

Helen Banderos is an Assistant Forensic Practitioner with London's Metropolitan Police Service. Her day, like other forensic investigators around the world, involves not only crime scene investigations, but paperwork as well. She sums up the importance of her reports by demonstrating their role in the larger investigation: "not only do I have to make sure that the evidence I have found goes off promptly to be dealt with by the right departments. But I must also make sure that my colleagues starting on the other shifts know what I have done during the day and what I have found."[55]

For forensic video analysts, their reports need to meet all of the above, and more. As with any forensic science, video analysis has acronyms and jargon that are little known outside the community. A post-analysis report that is indecipherably filled with references to frames, codecs, and algorithms is likely to be of little help to a detective, a prosecuting attorney, a defense attorney, or a jury.

Consequently, a video analysis report needs to be written in plain, straight-forward language, must be grammatically correct, and must be without spelling errors. In addition, as with the detectives investigating the crime, the report needs

An important part of a forensic video analyst job is the ability to write reports concerning his or her daily activities.

EASTERN DISTRICT

DAILY CAMERA ACTIVITY REPORT

JUNE 2006

"We're In The Money!"

Surveillance cameras on busses and subway trains have led to a decrease in fraudulent claims against transportation companies.

Mass transit companies have installed video surveillance cameras on buses and trains to ensure the safety of passengers and staff, but the cameras have also had one unintended consequence: fraud protection.

Digital cameras linked with on-board microphones have caught a number of individuals who thought they could claim that an injury was incurred during their trip. In Florida, a city bus had a minor collision with a parked bus; while most of the passengers exited the bus unharmed, a number of them stayed behind and talked with one another about how they were going to sue and collect damages.

William Sorrells, manager of the Safety and Training Department for Broward County Transit, recalls watching the video of the accident's aftermath, which included some of them singing, "We're In The Money!": "I'm watching this video, and I see all of these people connive with one another to go to their lawyer or their chiropractor or doctor, and they're going to do this and that. And [I hear them say], 'Oh, man, we're going to be rich!' How do you think that turned out in court?"

William Sorrells quoted in Lindsay Isaacs, "Transit surveillance: Wrecks, lies and videotape," *American City & County*, January 1, 2003. http://americancityandcounty.com/mag/government_transit_surveillance_wrecks/.

to avoid a prejudicial point of view. LEVA's Code of Ethics guidelines for its members counsels that the analyst "shall always be objective and impartial when conducting forensic video analysis and in the preparation of all reports."[56]

Because these reports play an important part in the decision process concerning how the case will be pursued, the entire report must demonstrate the analyst's professionalism, and must be consistent with the policies and practices of the examiner's agency or department. For example, Minneapolis, Minnesota, Police Department staff members must enter each report into an automated database called CAPRS, or Computer Assisted Police Records System, that the department has used to archive reports since 1990. Detectives and prosecuting attorneys use the report's information, along with the other evidence in the case, to decide how to proceed against the suspect or suspects. In more and more cases, the report's findings and the analyzed video determine the next step in the investigation.

"That Kind of Shot Their Defense"

For many investigators, surveillance video evidence can be a tremendous tool during the inquiry phase of a crime investigation. As Kansas City Police Detective Steve Morgan puts it, while every case is different, "video can be used as leverage in an investigation."[57] In other words, it can be used as a demonstration of what the investigators plan to use in the prosecution of the case, when interrogating suspects or when meeting with defense attorneys.

Some evidence leads to speedier results. For Criminalist Hisey, the de-multiplexed video of the bar assault led to a meeting between the prosecuting attorney in the case and the suspect's defense attorney. Her work with the video allowed her to create a presentation package that isolated one camera of the system to tell the story. The prosecutor played the video, which showed the accused in the middle of the fight. The evidence "kind of shot their defense [and] the defendant ended up taking a plea bargain."[58] Without it, the accusations and denials would likely have resulted in the entire matter being re-visited in a court case.

Other investigators have had similar experiences. For CSI Pilkington, numerous cases have not gone to trial as a result of the presentation of video evidence in a conference between the prosecution and the defense. Recalling the cases in which he has been involved, when surveillance video contained enough information to be used by the prosecution, "everyone who has been confronted with the video has plea bargained."[59] Brett Hallgren, of the Vancouver Police Department, says that, in his experience, ninety-five percent of the cases in which video evidence is presented before a trial results in guilty pleas.

Resolving cases in this manner undoubtedly saves time for both the police departments and the court systems. Prosecuting attorneys need not go to court for what could be a lengthy trial; court systems have fewer trials on their calendars; and detectives and other members of law enforcement agencies need not take time from their other duties to appear for testimony. The local governments also save money; according to Vicki Long, of the Alameda County, California, District Attorney's Office: "if we can get a case to plead out, it's definitely a big monetary savings for the county overall."[60]

However, in cases that do go to trial, the investigators need to be prepared to explain exactly what they have done to obtain the video evidence. Their forensic analysis reports must also be useful for future reference, as an investigator may be called upon to testify in court about what steps he or she performed on a piece of video months or even years after the crime occurred.

Such occasions are an opportunity to explain and display exactly what the video evidence shows. However, more and more frequently, analysts and prosecuting attorneys discover what they call "the CSI effect" affecting how technology and evidence is perceived by the public and potential jurors, as well as by suspects and defense attorneys.

"They Expect It to Look Like It Does on Television"

There has been a tremendous upswing in interest in the forensic sciences in the early twenty-first century. University programs that offer forensic science curricula are having a difficult time keeping up with the demand. The interest is due, in part, to the popularity of the television show *CSI: Crime Scene Investigation*, and others like it. Viewers see scientists and crime scene investigators working hand-in-hand with detectives and prosecutors to obtain usable evidence from seemingly impossible conditions, using all manner of sophisticated techniques and high-tech machines. These accomplishments, seen by millions of viewers, have created what law enforcement personnel call "the CSI effect." LEVA defines it bluntly as

Television shows, like CSI: Crime Scene Investigation *have created what law enforcement officials call "the 'CSI' effect."*

91

The unreasonable expectations about the capabilities of crime scene technicians and forensic scientists to always find and analyze physical evidence in an impossibly short period of time. This unreasonable expectation is based on the public's observations of over-dramatized depictions of forensic capabilities in a television show called "CSI."[61]

Prosecutors and officers discover that potential and seated jurors now expect the high-tech tools seen on television to be applied to every case.

Unfortunately, not all that is shown on these television programs is actually possible in real life. Detective Morgan chuckles at some of the forensic video capabilities of the CSIs on television. Discussing one scene in which a vital clue from a video was extracted from a reflection on a pair of sunglasses in a crowd, he summed up the chances of that happening in real life as unlikely: "given the resolution of today's cameras, that's just not possible."[62]

Detective Morgan is not alone. Other individuals in law enforcement and prosecution believe that the genre of shows is having an impact on potential jurors. Josh Marquis, the District Attorney in Astoria, Oregon, notes, "they expect us to have the most advanced technology possible, and they expect it to look like it does on television."[63] The realities of under-funded departments and laboratories with outdated equipment clash with the images on the television screen, and the prosecutors strive to inject reality into each case that may involve forensic evidence.

The CSI effect undoubtedly affects cases in which video is used as evidence against a suspect. Before the current generation of software became available, law enforcement officials were hampered by equipment standards and restrictions, and testimony and demonstrations in court were less effective than they are today.

"We Know How Powerful It Can Be"

Presenting surveillance video evidence in court without having analyzed the footage with the latest software tools can have a significant bearing on the case. For example, demonstrating evidence from a multiplexed video on a standard video playback unit is practically impossible. Jonathan Hak, a Crown Prosecutor for Alberta Justice in the Province of Alberta, says that before the latest forensic video tools reached the market, "I would put the video in the VCR and hit play, and tell the judge, 'Look! See? See?' and that was it. We couldn't see anything more than we could see with a cursory [superficial] view of the video."[64]

A CCTV operator monitors a possible drug deal in Baltimore, Maryland. The latest surveillance systems have led prosecutors to place more trust in the use of video as evidence at trials.

Consequently, the latest generation of forensic video tools means that law enforcement personnel have an increased confidence in the effectiveness of surveillance video in crime scene investigations and prosecutions. The latest tools mean that prosecutors place more trust in the use of video as evidence that all parties can understand. In addition, forensic video analysts have a greater sense of accomplishment concerning their video work.

The increased use of surveillance systems throughout the business and government communities, as well as the advanced tools available to the investigators, has led to an interesting trend among analysts. Because of their skills, and because of the number of plea bargains reached between prosecutors and defense attorneys, few forensic video analysts get called to court.

CSI Pilkington recalls that he has gone to court in relation to other cases, but has not testified in any cases related to his video work. Eddie Burns, a forensic video analyst for the Chandler, Arizona, Police Department, recalled that, "Of the 250 cases that I have worked, I have yet to go to court."[65] Jason Latham, who works as a forensic video analyst for the Johnson County, Kansas, Sheriff's Department's Criminalistics Laboratory, said that he had only been called to testify four times in 150 cases. Constable Brian Anderson, of the Edmonton, Alberta, Police Service, expresses a bit of disappointment in not being able to present his team's video expertise in court: "in most cases, after we've prepared a disclosure package to both defense and prosecuting attorneys, we do end up hearing that the result was a guilty plea. We often look forward to going to court with these cases and presenting our evidence because we know how powerful it can be."[66]

In those cases that do go to trial, the forensic video analyst needs to be able to articulate what has been done to enhance the video in a clear and concise manner, and also needs to understand how to deal with cross-examination.

On the Stand

Grant Fredericks, an independent forensic video consultant, previously worked for the Vancouver, British Columbia, Police Department and currently serves as an instructor for LEVA. Having reviewed hundreds of cases involving video, Fredericks is recognized as an expert of, and a pioneer in, the field of forensic video analysis.

As part of the LEVA course, "Advanced Forensic Video Analysis and the Law," Fredericks and Crown Prosecutor Hak put the course attendees through simulated courtroom proceedings. They assess the participants' speaking skills, their demeanor, and their ability to defend their video analysis. Fredericks takes the role of defense attorney, and is very convincing.

After one such exercise, forensic video analyst Latham recalled his experience on the stand. "Grant Fredericks just absolutely grilled you on the cases and evaluated how well you processed this case and how well you defend what you know about video in a courtroom environment."[67] Analyst Burns added that, if you could handle a cross-examination from Fredericks, "then you could probably handle a cross-examination from any defense attorney in the country."[68]

Analysts are called to the witness stand to defend their video work for a variety of reasons. Defense attorneys wish to place doubts in the jurors' minds that the video actually shows what the prosecutors contend. They ask about how the video information was retrieved and how it was stored. These

A forensic video analyst testifying in court. Analysts are often called to the witness stand to defend their work.

questions reinforce why complete documentation throughout the process is essential. The analyst's documentation—photographs of the crime scene and of the video system before, during, and after the surveillance footage is extracted, as well as notes of the system's status and records that show standard operating procedures for secure storage were followed—must support the analyst's testimony.

Defense attorneys may also call into question how the video was manipulated. The analyst must be able to demonstrate that adjustments made for color balance and luminance did not affect the content of the evidence, or that artifacts present in the duplicate footage that is used as evidence were present in the original.

In addition, the defense may raise the question of compression, claiming that vital information is lost through compression and decompression, and that this might lead to a misidentification of a suspect. The analyst must be able to demonstrate that the techniques used in the extraction process addressed these issues. In response to compression concerns, many of the latest software applications enable analysts to work with the uncompressed DME, which will lend further credibility to the analyst's testimony.

The latest tools, the increasing quality of video footage, and the ability to create presentation packages that show the evidence clearly and efficiently, seem to be relegating the forensic video analyst to serving as an expert witness only if necessary. Accounts of trials in which surveillance footage plays an important role now feature prosecutors presenting and explaining the video evidence, without any explanations of the efforts that were involved in retrieving, preserving, and analyzing the data.

Prosecutors Putting It All Together

In 2003, Crown Prosecutor Hak recalled a case he had presented, stemming from a murder that had occurred in a back alley. The murder itself was not caught on video, but important activity that took place just ten minutes later was. Surveillance video from a nearby convenience store showed two men driving up, entering, making a purchase, and leaving.

These two men were investigated in connection with the murder. The victim's DNA was found on the left side of the driver's seat of the car that the two men used, but it was not known which one had been the driver. Hak recounted that the surveillance video from the convenience store played an important part in the case. The latest generation of forensic video tools allowed the analysts to "look beyond the front window of the store into the darkness, and by tracking pixels, we were able to determine who the driver of the car was."[69]

Hak noted that determining which of the men was the driver gave them an important piece to the puzzle. Because the murderer had the victim's DNA on him, he would have deposited the DNA on a car seat when he re-entered the vehicle. Knowing that the victim's DNA was found on the driver's side, and then knowing which of the men was the driver, the prosecution was confident in identifying which of the two men was the murderer.

In 2005, Raymond F. Morrogh, Deputy Commonwealth Attorney for Fairfax County, Virginia, presented a case connected with a shootout between a robbery suspect and a police officer. The suspect had entered a check-cashing store and asked the clerk if the store had a surveillance system. While he looked around for the cameras, the clerk pressed a silent alarm notification button, alerting the police. When the officer arrived, the suspect emerged from the store, pulled out a gun, and started firing.

Security personnel, who were actively monitoring a surveillance system at a U.S. federal government building across the street, heard the gunfire. They panned and zoomed their rooftop camera toward the confrontation, thereby catching the crime as it occurred.

Morrogh played the video for the court and the jury, calling it "the cherry on top"[70] of his case. In the video clip, the court and jury saw the suspect and the officer exchange shots before the officer, a former U.S. Marine Corps sharpshooter, wounded the suspect with a shot as he tried to flee the scene. After Morrogh confronted the suspect on the witness stand with the pictures, the jury found the defendant guilty of attempted capital murder, due in part to the action caught on the surveillance video.

"Nothing But Positive Reviews"

Since the 1960s, entirely new fields of forensic science have evolved. Investigators take for granted such advances as DNA analysis, fiber analysis, mass spectrometry, gas chromatography, and fingerprint databases. Now, the capabilities of the forensic video analyst are catching up with the advances in motion picture photography. The analyst now has the ability to extract, study, and present the video's information in an effective and accurate form that everyone can understand.

The role of surveillance video has already changed the way crime scenes are investigated. If the business or area where the crime occurred has no security cameras, the chances are that there are a few in the immediate vicinity. Law enforcement officers routinely now look for cameras for blocks surrounding a crime scene; Crown Prosecutor Hak believes that many will canvass an area up to a mile (1.6km) from the site in search of clues caught by cameras.

In addition, as with other forensic sciences, such as fingerprinting and DNA, the use of surveillance video as evidence has become more accepted in the courtroom. Judges and juries are becoming more accustomed to surveillance video being offered as evidence, especially if the pictures are clear, the color is lifelike, and the action is easy to follow. As Officer Brett Hallgren puts it, "for those cases that have gone to court, there have been nothing but positive reviews by the judges" concerning the video evidence produced with the latest forensic tools.

Expanding technologies will likely affect video surveillance systems of the future. Two-camera systems that mimic human

A New Lab for the Future of Forensic Video Training

In February 2007, with law enforcement officers from around the world on hand, the University of Indianapolis and the Law Enforcement & Emergency Services Video Association unveiled the Digital Multimedia Evidence Processing Laboratory, the first of its kind in the field. The laboratory combines state-of-the-art equipment with a permanent, university-based training facility.

The lab grew out a partnership between Professor Thomas Christenberry, the University's director of public safety education, and LEVA. Christenberry spent twenty-five years with the FBI, which included training special agents and law enforcement personnel at the FBI's Quantico, Virginia, facility, before becoming director of public safety education at the university. The university hosted a number of LEVA courses from 2004 to 2007 before the new lab was established. The lab has the capacity to train up to thirty-eight investigators at a time, and will enable students to apply classroom learning through video editing, simulations, and other hands-on experiences.

Jan Garvin, vice president for forensic video training with LEVA, looked forward to the enhanced partnership with the university: "we stress the value of agencies integrating forensic video analysis into their investigative arsenals. The university's cooperation, enthusiasm and commitment to this project already have resulted in a tremendous impact to the global law enforcement community."

Jan Garvin, quoted in University of Indianapolis, "UIndy unveils forensic video lab," February 26, 2007. http://www.uindy.edu/news/?p=419.

Video cameras are not only found at businesses anymore, they are often found in neighborhoods. Law enforcement officials often look at these cameras as well when investigating a crime.

sight may become the standard. Systems are already being developed that capture potentially hazardous activity and that alert monitors to the events. Some systems in Great Britain use interactive video, in which personnel who monitor active surveillance systems can provide feedback to those they observe through the use of loudspeakers near the cameras. It remains to be seen how these innovations will be received by the public and by the courts in future investigations.

For now, crime scene investigators will continue to look for cameras at the scene of the crime. They will continue to hope that a surveillance system there or nearby will yield an important clue to their case. Perhaps it will help reunite lost or abducted children with their parents, or identify a bank robber or murder suspect, or, perhaps, as with Carlie Brucia, catch someone in the act.

"It's All About Justice"

For the investigators and prosecutors involved with Carlie Brucia's abduction and murder, the car wash surveillance footage was a key piece to their case. Their forensic video analysis revealed important clues related to her disappearance. Releasing the video to the public led law enforcement personnel to investigate, and eventually arrest, Joseph P. Smith. His subsequent confession led them to where he had buried Carlie. The video was shown by the prosecution and by the media repeatedly during Smith's trial, as well as following his conviction for Carlie's murder. He was found guilty by a Florida jury and sentenced to death by a judge in December 2005.

Carlie's case reinforces that the study of surveillance videos in crime scene investigations is like any other forensic science. It requires the proper tools, but it also requires the creativity of the analyst's experience and dedication to bring to light all the information a video contains. The challenge for crime scene investigators will be to understand and to adapt to new situations and new technologies, so that they can continue accurately and objectively to provide law enforcement agencies with the best evidence possible.

For CSI Mitch Pilkington, the forensic sciences provide him with a particular certainty about crime scene investigations. For example, either a fingerprint matches, or it doesn't. In his video work, the footage either shows an individual or an action, or it doesn't. He recalls cases that he has helped investigate that has attracted media attention, such as murders, and others, such as car thefts or vandalism, that were only important to the individuals involved. For him, it matters little how significant the case may be. Summing up his role, he says, "a lot of the work isn't pretty, but it does have its rewards. I'm looking to help right a wrong. It's all about justice."[71]

Notes

Chapter 1: "The Video Might Be Your Only Witness"

1. Telephone interview, Detective Steve Morgan, May 15, 2007.

2. Chris Bristol, "Man faces prison for stealing memorial," *Yakima Herald-Republic,* April 12, 2007.

3. B. J. Goould, quoted in Jerry Ratcliffe, *Problem-Oriented Guides for Police: Response Guides Series No. 4: Video Surveillance of Public Places* (Washington, DC: U.S. Department of Justice, Office of Community Oriented Policing Services, 2006), p. 3.

4. Quoted in Michael E. Ruane, "Security Camera New Star Witness," *Washington Post,* October 8, 2005, p. B-1.

5. Ratcliffe, p. 4.

6. Ratcliffe, p. 22.

7. Telephone interview, Professor Thomas Christenberry, May 9, 2007.

8. Alan C. Bovik, "Introduction to Digital Image and Video Processing," in Al Bovik (editor), *Handbook of Image & Video Processing,* San Diego: Academic Press, 2000, p. 5.

9. Telephone interview, Detective Steve Morgan, May 16, 2007.

10. Telephone interview, Crime Scene Investigator Mitch Pilkington, May 21, 2007.

11. Bovik, p. 3.

12. Scott Anderson, "Bit by Bit—Digital Takes Over," Videomaker.com, September 1999, http://www.videomaker.com/article/7287/.

13. Anderson, "Bit by Bit—Digital Takes Over."

14. Telephone interview, Professor Thomas Christenberry, May 9, 2007.

15. Boyd Bryant, "What Alarm and Video Surveillance Isn't: More Cameras, Fewer Watchers," Officer.com, April 30, 2007, http://www.officer.com/article/article.jsp?siteSection=20 &id=35911.

16. Quoted in Julie Scheeres, "Video Forensics: Grainy to Guilty," *Wired Magazine,* January 30, 2002, http://www.wired.com/politics/law/news/2002/01/50036.

17. Frost & Sullivan, *North American IP Video Surveillance Storage Markets,* February 2007, quoted in "Ramping up of Security in Airport and Gaming Sectors Boosts Adoption of IP Video Surveillance in North America," *Business Wire Magazine,* April 16, 2007.

Chapter 2: Collecting the Evidence

18. Lt. Brian McNulty, quoted in "Two arrested in elderly purse snatching," My Fox Tampa Bay, May 21, 2007, http://www.myfoxtampabay.com/myfox/pages/Home/Detail;jsessionid=44A742C0B6A76A9A37352EE4C27A393E?contentId=3269949&version=2&locale=EN-US&layoutCode=TSTY&pageId=1.1.1&sflg=1.

19. Telephone interview, Detective Morgan, May 16, 2007.

20. LEVA DME Team, "Best Practices for the Acquisition of Digital Multimedia Evidence," March 2007, p. 9. http://www.leva.org/pdf/BestPracticesDigitalMultimediaEvidence.pdf.

21. Telephone interview, Professor Thomas Christenberry, May 9, 2007.

22. LEVA DME Team, "Best Practices for the Acquisition of Digital Multimedia Evidence," p. 9.

23. Telephone interview, Detective Morgan, May 16, 2007.

24. LEVA DME Team, "Best Practices for the Acquisition of Digital Multimedia Evidence," p. 9.

25. Telephone interview, CSI Pilkington, May 21, 2007.

26. LEVA DME Team, "Best Practices for the Acqustion of Digital Multimedia Evidence," p. 3.

27. Telephone Interview, CSI Pilkington, May 21, 2007.

28. Telephone Interview, CSI Pilkington, May 21, 2007.

29. Detective Bill Coakley, quoted in Kevin Gordon, "Video Forensics Tools," Law and Order, April 2006. Available at www.hendonpub.com/publications/lawandorder/otherfeaturedarticles.asp?ID=605.

30. LEVA DME Team, "Best Practices for the Acquisition of Digital Multimedia Evidence," p. 12.

31. Telephone Interview, CSI Pilkington, May 21, 2007.

Chapter 3: Forensic Video Analysis

32. Metropolitan Police Service, "Important information about CCTV," May 2006. http://www.met.police.uk/ crimeprevention/cctv.htm.

33. Brett Hallgren, quoted in "dTective Customer Testimonials," 2000. http://www.oceansystems.com/dtective/customers.htm.

34. Telephone interview, CSI Pilkington, June 3, 2007.

35. Personal interview, Jay Gelber, April 14, 2007, Fairbanks, Alaska.

36. Telephone interview, Detective Morgan, May 16, 2007.

37. Personal interview, Jay Gelber, April 14, 2007, Fairbanks, Alaska.

38. Personal interview, Jay Gelber, April 14, 2007, Fairbanks, Alaska.

39. Telephone interview, CSI Pilkington, April 24, 2007.

40. Criminalist Shelli Hisey, quoted in "dTective Customer Testimonials," 2002. http://www.oceansystems.com/dtective/customers.htm.

41. Detective Bill Coakley, quoted in Gordon, "Video Forensics Tools."

42. Criminalist Hisey, quoted in "dTective Customer Testimonials."

43. Telephone interview, CSI Pilkington, April 24, 2007.

44. Grant Fredericks, quoted in James Careless, "Analyze This," Government Video.com, May 22, 2006. http://governmentvideo.com/articles/publish/article_884.shtml.

45. Telephone interview, Detective Morgan, May 15, 2007.

Chapter 4: A Team Effort

46. Telephone interview, CSI Pilkington, May 21, 2007.

47. Criminalist Hisey, quoted in "dTective Customer Testimonials."

48. Scientific Working Group on Imaging Technology, "Best Practices for Forensic Image Analysis," January 11, 2007, p. 3. Available at http://www.theiai.org/guidelines/swgit/guidelines/section_12_v1-6.pdf.

49. Telephone interview, Detective Morgan, May 15, 2007.

50. Telephone interview, CSI Pilkington, April 24, 2007.

51. David Krejicek, "It's Joe Smith," in *Notorious Murders/Most Famous: The Abduction of Carlie Brucia*, 2007. http://www.crimelibrary.com/notorious_murders/famous/carlie_brucia/4.html.

52. Staff Sgt. Jorge Lasso, quoted in TechWeb, "YouTube Helps Canadian Police Find Murder Suspect," December 21, 2006. www.darkreading.com/document.asp?doc_id=113348.

53. Telephone interview, CSI Pilkington, April 24, 2007.

54. "Precinct News," *MNPD Newsline*, March 9, 2007, p. 5.

Chapter 5: Evidence All Can Understand

55. "Specialist Crime Directorate: a day in the life of an Assistant Forensic Practitioner," n.d. http://www.met.police.uk/scd/specialist_units/day_in_the_life.htm.

56. LEVA, "Code of Ethics: Forensic Video Analysis," 2007.

57. Telephone interview, Detective Morgan, May 16, 2007.

58. Criminalist Hisey, quoted in "dTective Customer Testimonials."

59. Telephone interview, CSI Pilkington, April 24, 2007.

60. Vicki Long, quoted in "dTective Customer Testimonials," 2003. http://www.oceansystems.com/dtective/customers.htm.

61. Robert C. Sanders et. al., "Forensic Imaging and Multi-media Glossary," July 15, 2006, p. 59. Available at www.leva.org/pdf/GlossaryV7.pdf.

62. Telephone interview, Detective Morgan, May 15, 2007.

63. Quoted in Vince Gonzales, "Prosecutors Feel the 'CSI Effect,'" CBS News, February 10, 2005. www.cbsnews.com/ stories/2005/02/10/eveningnews/main673060.shtml.

64. Crown Prosecutor Jonathan Hak, quoted in "dTective Customer Testimonials," 2003. http://www.oceansystems.com/dtective/customers.htm.

65. Quoted in Kristi Mayo, "Forensic Video Analysis: Training and certification help video analysts approach their jobs with a new level of confidence," *Evidence Technology Magazine,* September–October 2005, p. 39.

66. Constable Brian Anderson, quoted in "dTective Customer Testimonials," 2003. http://www.oceansystems.com/dtective/customers.htm.

67. Quoted in Mayo, "Forensic Video Analysis: Training and certification help video analysts approach their jobs with a new level of confidence," p. 38.

68. Quoted in Mayo, "Forensic Video Analysis: Training and certification help video analysts approach their jobs with a new level of confidence," p. 38.

69. Crown Prosecutor Jonathan Hak, quoted in "dTective Customer Testimonials," 2003.

70. Quoted in Michael E. Ruane, "Security Camera New Star Witness," *Washington Post,* October 8, 2005, p. B-1.

71. Telephone interview, CSI Pilkington, June 14, 2007.

Glossary

active surveillance: A video surveillance system that is continually monitored by personnel who are assigned to that one task.

algorithm: A step-by-step procedure for solving an often-repeated problem or accomplishing some mathematical function, especially by a computer. In forensic video analysis, an algorithm is often found at the heart of compression/decompression techniques developed by video recording manufacturers.

analog video recording: Similar to film camera photography, analog video recording captures the image directly on the videotape.

artifact: A visual aberration in a video recording resulting from a technical or operational limitation. Examples include speckles or blocks, changes in luminance, or changes in color balance.

CCTV: Short for Closed-Circuit Television. Originally referred to a system in which video was transmitted within a closed network, as opposed to public broadcasting. Current usage refers to any type of video surveillance system.

codec: Short for compression/decompression. The algorithm that dictates the amount of compression a video signal undergoes during recording, and the method of recompression the signal undergoes at playback.

covert surveillance: A system of surveillance cameras that is fully hidden from the public.

criminalist: A member of a law enforcement department who collects physical evidence at crime scenes and receives evidence at the laboratory, performing and/or overseeing or supervising the chemical and/or physical analyses of samples collected as evidence.

CSI: Short for Crime Scene Investigator. A member of a law enforcement department who specializes in collecting and documenting evidence at a crime scene, including (but not limited to) fingerprint, bloodstain, and video surveillance evidence.

CSI effect: A term coined by law enforcement personnel that refers to citizens' and jurors' expectations concerning crime scene investigation and technology capabilities, based on techniques presented by television shows such as *CSI: Crime Scene Investigation*.

digital video recording: Similar to digital audio recording, digital video recording captures the image as a binary signal.

discrete cosine transform: A process by which video information is compressed for recording or playback, based on mathematical algorithms.

DME: Short for Digital Multimedia Evidence. The assemblage of files associated with digital information from surveillance video cameras.

DVR: Short for Digital Video Recorder. A device that records video on to digital videotape or directly on to a computer hard drive.

forensic video analysis: The scientific examination, comparison, and/or evaluation of video.

interlacing: A method of capturing surveillance images on alternating odd and even horizontal lines of video information. One camera's information is displayed on the odd-numbered lines; another camera's information is displayed on the even-numbered lines.

lossy compression: Compression method in which data is lost through compression and cannot be restored through decompression.

luminance: The perceived brightness component of a given color, as opposed to its hue or its saturation.

overt surveillance: A system of surveillance cameras that is fully visible to the public.

passive surveillance: A video surveillance system that is not monitored by full-time personnel.

pixel: An individual element that, combined with others, creates an electronic image, such as on a television or computer screen. The word is a combination of "pix" (short for "pictures") and the first syllable of "element."

quad-screen: A type of multiplexing in which each camera's information is recorded on one quarter of each frame of film.

semi-covert surveillance: A system of surveillance cameras that is partially visible to the public, usually through the use of camera housings that conceal the contents.

still: An image captured from a video recording by pausing or halting the video, and copying the information from the screen.

VTR: Short for Videotape Recorder. A device that records video on to cassette tapes. Also called "video cassette recorder" or VCR.

working copy: A duplicate of the information of the surveillance video's footage in as complete a form as possible.

For More Information

Books:

Douglas P. Lyle, *Forensics for Dummies*. Foster City, California: IDG Books Worldwide, 2004. A comprehensive yet accessible guide to the field of forensics.

Jerry Ratcliffe, *Problem-Oriented Guides for Police: Response Guides Series No. 4: Video Surveillance of Public Places*. Washington, DC: U.S. Department of Justice, Office of Community Oriented Policing Services, 2006. An overview of the different types of surveillance systems.

Periodicals:

Azam Ahmed, "Captured on video but not by police: Unlike TV, evidence isn't always enough," *Chicago Tribune*, May 14, 2007. This article addresses the premise that continued releases of crime scene videos may not aid law enforcement efforts as the public becomes more and more disinterested in the footage.

Scott Anderson, "Bit by Bit—Digital Takes Over," *Videomaker*, September 1999. An imaginary dialogue between the author and his "mentor," with some very useful information about the differences between analog and digital video formats.

Gary Gulick, "Compression Standard: Most forensic video analysts say they would like to see an industry standard for digital video," *Evidence Technology Magazine*, September–October 2005. An examination of the challenges posed by analyzing videos with a variety of compression formats and techniques.

Jeffrey Kluger, "How Science Solves Crimes," *Time*, October 21, 2002. A fascinating account of the rise of forensic science in popularity on television and its use in the courtroom.

Kristi Mayo, "Forensic Video Analysis: Training and certification help video analysts approach their jobs with a new level of confidence," *Evidence Technology Magazine*, September–October 2005. A look at the behind the scenes training session conducted by the Law Enforcement & Emergency Services Video Association.

Amanda Ripley, "Facing Facts in America," *Time*, July 11, 2005. Article documents security changes after 9/11, including the installation of video surveillance in Washington, D.C.'s subway system.

Michael E. Ruane, "Security Camera New Star Witness: Detectives Mining a Wealth of Evidence," *Washington Post*, October 8, 2005. Excellent article that documents how one surveillance video was used to capture a crime in progress, and how it was used effectively in the courtroom.

Internet Sources:

CNN, "Housemate tips police to Smith after seeing video," February 6, 2004. (http://www.cnn.com/2004/US/South/02/05/missing.girl/). Account of the effectiveness of the decision to release the Evie's Car Wash video to the public.

DarkReading, "YouTube Helps Canadian Police Find Murder Suspect," December 21, 2006. (www.darkreading.com/document.asp?doc_id=113348). Account of how the Hamilton, Ontario, police used YouTube.com to nab a suspect.

National Public Radio, "Computers Sort Files to Find Criminals," *All Things Considered*, April 20, 2007. (http://www.npr.org/templates/story/story.php?storyId=9724348). Examination of the uses and evolution of surveillance video databases.

Web Sites:

Court TV's Crime Library's Examination of the Carlie Brucia Case (http://www.crimelibrary.com/notorious_murders/famous/carlie_brucia/1.html). This section of the site examines not only the case, but also its aftermath.

Court TV's Crime Library's Examination of the James Bulger Case (http://www.crimelibrary.com/notorious_murders/young/bulger/1.html). A comprehensive overview of the case, including updates about the major players in the case ten years after the murder.

Court TV's Crime Library's Examination of the Dr. David Cornbleet Case (http://www.crimelibrary.com/news/original/0107/0103_cornbleet_murder.html). Excellent background of the case, as well as an examination of the video evidence.

The Federal Bureau of Investigation's Regional Computer Forensic Labs (RCFLs) (http://www.rcfl.gov/). This main page for the RCFL program provides background information and links to the regional RCFLs throughout the US.

The International Association for Identification (IAI) (http://www.theiai.org/). This organization consists of individuals involved in various types of forensic identification occupations, including forensic video analysis. The site includes excellent links to forensic identification guides as well as an RSS feed for job openings.

The International Association of Chiefs of Police (IACP) (http://www.theiacp.org/). An excellent starting point for a career in law enforcement, as well as links to publications featuring stories about evolving trends in police work, including car cams, digital video, and video forensics.

**The Law Enforcement & Emergency
Services Video Association (LEVA)**
(http://www.leva.org/). LEVA is a
leading association for individuals in the
video analysis field, and offers a certification program run by some of the top
investigators in the field.

Index

Picture Credits

About the Author

Andrew A. Kling worked for the National Park Service for over fifteen years in locations throughout the United States. He now works as a writer and editor for a variety of non-profit organizations, and as an interpretive media developer and consultant. He enjoys hockey, technology, vexillology, and spending time with his wife and their famous Norwegian Forest cat, Chester.